PIÑON COUNTRY

LIBRARY

WITHDRAWN

MAY 1 5 2020

UNBC Library

LIBRARY

PIÑON
COUNTRY

Haniel Long

Foreword by Tony Hillerman

University of Nebraska Press
Lincoln and London

Copyright 1941 by Haniel Long
Renewal copyright 1969 by Anton V. Long
Foreword copyright 1986 by the University of Nebraska Press
All rights reserved
Manufactured in the United States of America

First Bison Book printing: 1986
Most recent printing indicated by the first digit below
1   2   3   4   5   6   7   8   9   10

Library of Congress Cataloging-in-Publication Data

Long, Haniel, 1888–1956.
Piñon country.

Reprint. Originally published: New York: Duell,
Sloan & Pearce, c1941.
Includes index.
1. Southwest, New — History. 2. Southwest, New —
Description and travel. 3. Indians of North America —
Southwest, New. I. Title.
F786.L8 1986   978.9   86-4309
ISBN 0-8032-7919-1 (pbk.)

Reprinted by arrangement with Anton V. Long,
for the estate of Haniel Long

Originally published in 1941 by Duell, Sloan & Pearce

Southwest Review published "Printing in the Southwest" which, with their permission and that of the Southwestern Library Association, is here republished in part as "Pioneer Presses." My theory about Coronado and his accident appeared in longer form in *The New Mexico Quarterly* under the title "The Man Coronado."

To friends in or out of my book who have shared what they know of life in the piñon country and so given me more of it than I could ever gain by myself—and to the friend, too, who told me to write the book

Contents

The Upper Sonoran life-belt is a world of its own. Among the dwarf trees, water is scarce and people have always had to plan together about sharing it:

The first Europeans to reach the Upper Sonoran had trouble continuing to be European. Each in his own way had to face the need of sharing. They give us our first picture of the Pueblo Indians:

The Spanish colonists found it a hard land to live in, though the Crown helped them. When we came we did not help them. To remember it is to understand much of the society and politics of New Mexico:

Contents

Some people could move into the Southwest and live long lives without killing Indians or being killed by them:

Colonists from the States started newspapers wherever they went. It may have been from the same instinct that produced the Town Meeting back East:

Canyons, caverns, walking red rain, great rocks like ships, or covered wagons on the horizon are part of the inheritance of the region, and visitors come in ever greater numbers:

Young Indians everywhere are finding difficult their new life. Economically, the Navajo complain of the way we plan their future, and nobody can blame them:

Contents

Foreword

By Tony Hillerman

Piñon Country came to be in 1941 as part of a project that seems totally inconceivable in today's world of corporate conglomerate bottom-line publishing. Duell, Sloan & Pearce, Inc., the now-defunct publishing house then at 270 Madison Avenue, hired Erskine Caldwell as editor of "American Folkways" and signed contracts with some of the nation's most luminous literary figures. They were to produce books reflecting the life and culture of their favorite region. William Faulkner was signed up for *Piney Woods Country*, Louis Bromfield for *Buckeye Country*, and Harnett Kane for *Deep Delta Country*. Out of this project came some memorable Americana—including Wallace Stegner's *Mormon Country* and Edwin Corle's *Desert Country*. One of the first, and one of the best, was *Piñon Country*.

I confess I can only guess why Haniel Long was tapped to write *Piñon Country*, which was to deal with New Mexico and Arizona—the high end of the Sonoran Desert and the south side of the Colorado Plateau. Relatively speaking, he was a newcomer among the region's many writers. Long was an easterner, a minister's son born in Burma, raised in Pennsylvania, educated in the silver-spoon, old-family, Anglo-elitist tradition of Exeter and Harvard. He'd spent two decades of his life teaching literature at Carnegie Tech in his hometown of Pittsburgh. He'd come to Santa Fe only in 1929, one of the multitude who sought the high, dry air in interests of health. The handicap of being a newcomer shows now and then in the text.

Fortunately, other things also show. One is Long's talent as a writer—his ability to produce simple, lucid prose and to use warm and human anecdotes as the backbone of many of his essays. Another is his convert's affection for the land and for the cultures that had developed in its mountain villages, in the pueblos along its rivers, and in the eroded waste of Navajo Country.

Long had experienced his first real immersion in the Piñon Country he was to write about by a happy accident. The year was 1920. Long and his wife and child were returning to Pittsburgh from Los Angeles, where he had considered moving to escape the smoke and grime of the steel mills. He was returning to Pennsylvania, disillusioned by California, when the train was delayed for two hours near Laguna Pueblo.

It is hard to imagine a place more likely to touch a person of Long's personality. He loved vast and dramatic landscapes and had an ever-deepening interest in the metaphysical side of human society. From where the train stopped, he would have seen the stone and adobe buildings of Old Laguna clustered atop their hill, crowned, like a medieval village, by the whitewashed shape of the pueblo church. To the west the old volcano we call Mount Taylor rises eleven thousand feet against the sky. The north is walled off by the cliffs of Mesa Chivata, the northeast by Mesa Gigante and far to the south he would have seen the land rolling away toward the blue shapes of Mesa del Oro and what we call the Acoma Buttes. It was—in fact still is—an ideal place to experience the incredible scale of landscape so characteristic of high desert country. Long told his friends later that in those two hours he fell in love with New Mexico.

Long wrote that he "felt like a giant" on that walk through the piñons with the mountains surrounding him. He returned to his teaching job at Carnegie Tech but he left his heart behind. Nine years later, at the urging of a friend, Santa Fe poet Witter Bynner, he came back to stay. He became a central figure in the writers' colony then flourishing in that odd little

mountain town—a colony that included Oliver LaFarge, Paul
Horgan, Mary Austin, Bynner, Roark Bradford, and others—
and in their cooperative effort, called Writers' Editions, which
published seventeen books before World War II put a stop to
such enterprises.

Long died in 1956, four years after I came to Santa Fe, and
was already losing his vision and his health when I arrived. I
knew him only by reputation. In *Southwest Classics,* Lawrence
Clark Powell calls him "a grave and kindly sage." Oliver
LaFarge described him to me as "a genuine rarity," a kind man,
a gentle man, a philosopher, who had, just below the surface, a
sublimated urge toward the wild and unconventional.
LaFarge's opinion seemed to express that of his contempo-
raries. Long's good friend Peggy Pond Church, in a superb ele-
giac poem, gives us a glimpse of him as part unicorn, uncom-
fortable in that role in an age that denies its mythology.

Piñon Country is valuable principally because it reflects
Long's personality and because, thanks to his skill, it lets us see
this part of the Southwest with his sensitive vision. It should be
read as a personal document, as the reflections of an intelligent, cultured man looking at this region, and looking at
almost fifty years ago. It should not be read as a reference.
Long's historical details have not all stood the test of time and
in some of his cultural comments he passes along misinforma-
tion. His essay on sandpainting stands as an excellent description of what he saw and what he was told. It should not be read
for any theological understanding of Navajo metaphysics. His
essay on the pioneer presses is another worthwhile contribution. But we now know that Josiah Gregg, and not Don Santiago Abreau, brought the first printing press into New Mexico, and Jack Rittenhouse, an acknowledged authority on the
subject, assures me that it was far too small to print the Cimarron newspaper. In other places, Long's essays suffer from
changing attitudes. I personally find hard to swallow Long's
admiration for Kit Carson, but Long was writing before Amer-

icans began looking for the feet of clay under their heroes. Long's statement "That Navajo live and multiply today is due largely to [Carson's] sense of brotherliness and hatred of unnecessary suffering" is ill-informed nonsense. Navajos remember Carson as a pretended friend who betrayed them, swept his troops through their territory, killing all who didn't escape, destroying their homes, cattle, and crops with a savage scorched-earth campaign worthy of Genghis Khan and then herding the survivors into captivity. But Long was writing before our consciousness (and our conscience) was raised on the subject of the white man's behavior and motivation in the frontier Indian wars. When he eulogizes Carson, or describes the decision of General Carleton to kill all male Apaches as being "as ruthless as the Indians," he reflected standard Anglo-American thinking of his time.

Aside from such quibbles, *Piñon Country* offers us an unusual opportunity to look at the New Mexico–Arizona high country as it was before World War II through the eyes of a man who loved it, and had the skill to describe it. When originally published, it drew good reviews. The *New York Times* said the book "gives one the kind of knowledge that one might have if one could drop in at a bull session of old-timers, smoking at ease, watching night come, unrestrained by the presence of the romantic or supercilious dude." It does, indeed, have that easy, anecdotal tone. And now there's the added delight of time travel. The bull session on which you're eavesdropping is almost a half-century old.

"He writes casually," said Stanley Walker in the *New York Herald Tribune*, "without passion or poetic passages, but he still manages to convey a great deal of the feel of this well-nigh inexplicable land." True again. The *New Yorker* called it "a superior performance, deftly written, intuitive and penetrating," and labeled it "a charming book."

It is a charming book because it reflects the mind of a charming man.

PIÑON COUNTRY

1. Water

MR. ISLEY: The state of Arizona is asking you for a portion of your water so we can have a maintenance camp on Highway 89 two miles inside the reservation boundary.

FRANK BRADLEY (*Navajo District 8*): We have been crowded all over the country for lack of water and we don't have enough water, and now he comes here and would corral that water we have on our land. Ten acres is a big piece of land, big enough to support a family.

WILLIAM GOODLUCK (*District 18*): At the last meeting there came before us for discussion the matter of a Navajo girl asking for a trading post on the highway. We thought it best not to give her a license. She was one of our people and we refused it. We are now being asked for an outsider to have some of our land. The water situation has affected us to a great extent. We don't have enough water for our stock. We are asked to give a portion of what little water we have for this gentleman. Looking at it that way I am not in favor of granting any permit to let go of any of that water.

—Minutes of the Navajo Tribal Council

A STATE highway engineer and two Navajo Indians talking at the Navajo Tribal Council at Window Rock, Arizona, in November, 1939, and you are face to face with the problem of the Southwest. If you lack

3

water, you are crowded all over the country. Ten acres of land that has water is a big piece, too big for you to allow anyone to corral it and take it away from you. You don't like to give any of it even to one of your own family. As it is you have to reduce your stock because of lack of water.

The limited supply circumscribes the present and the future of Pueblo, Navajo, Hopi, Apache, Spanish American, Mormon, everybody. Far more space in the daily paper goes to water than to any other subject. The news items about it are of all kinds. At Tesuque a one-armed native (in the Southwest the "natives" are the Spanish Americans) kills his neighbor (with a rifle, too) for stealing water. At Carlsbad the body of a prominent rancher is at the undertaker's and over the Texas line another prominent rancher is being held without bail—a "water-right argument." Governor Miles of New Mexico orders the state police to break the locks on the water gates in the Virden valley; farmers came to him crying their water was shut off so that Arizona Indians could irrigate. President Roosevelt signs a compact that ends a thirty years' dispute among the states of Texas, New Mexico, and Colorado for use of the waters of the Rio Grande. The Senate approves an additional appropriation of $500,000 for the dam and canal on the Rio Grande which divides waters apportioned the United States from those due Mexico. At Silver City the water superintendent warns everybody to use water sparingly. The weather man at Albuquerque says rain is needed over most lower elevation ranges, and soil is beginning to blow in the eastern dry-farming sections. A native named Sanchez sues the city of Albuquerque for four thousand dollars because a ditch overflowed into his home, and the jury disagrees over the justice of the claim. A three-year-old child at Pecos, Maria Barella, reaches too far out over a ditch for a floating stick, falls in, and is drowned.

It was a good neighbor named Rodriguez who first initiated me, the newcomer, into the world of water rights. A ditch comes down from the Acequia Madre (mother-ditch) through my garden and on to his. These ditches are communal and to enjoy their use you either have to work on them in the spring or pay the mayor-domo two dollars. Rodriguez introduced me to this official who presides over water. The mayor-domo is an old man named Padilla with a white straggly beard, and it is not so easy to find him as you might think. I have hunted him in all his favorite resorts about the plaza, and up and down the length of the big ditch, without result. When you do find him, the important thing is to agree on what morning or afternoon every week or two weeks you can have the water. With this agreed upon, you can go to the Acequia Madre and open up the gateway to your ditch, always provided somebody else has not made a mistake and thought it *his* time to get the water. Perhaps Padilla did not understand my pronunciation of the Spanish word for Tuesday? Or he did not remember it was to be Tuesday?

In Santa Fe the little ditches rarely run after the first of July. The supposition is that the rains will come and take care of you. But the rains do not always come on schedule, and it is a good fortune to have city water and a hose for the carrots and chard. I should not care to be a dry farmer, though the ditch is a good deal more exciting than the hose, of course. I know of nothing more pleasant than taking my shovel and going up the street at six o'clock on a May morning to the big ditch. Then, later, when I see the water in the little ditch coming under the fence onto my property I feel exhilarated. A native youth is much more expert in handling water than any newcomer could be—such a boy with his hoe will lead the water here and there with real skill. But when I have attempted it myself I have had fugitive impressions of a very different kind of life from any I have ever known, a much older one, in many ways a better one.

The amount of rainfall in the Southwest is largely a question of altitude. If you live between 3,000 and 4,500 feet above sea level, you get eight to ten inches. Between 4,500 and 6,000 feet, fifteen inches or thereabouts. From 7,000 feet on up, twenty to thirty inches. Cloudcroft, for example, at 9,000 feet gets twenty-four inches of water (including six feet of snow). An eastern city, like my native Pittsburgh, gets about forty-five inches.

New Mexico, Sonora, Arizona lie in a world zone of high pressure and consequent aridity. But the trade winds here are not assertive. In their place, fairly moist winds blow from the south. The interior of the continent in summer is an area of low pressure, for it is very hot, and the irregular winds move in toward this region across the southwest. Ellsworth Huntington, in his *Climatic Factor,* says of these winds, "They form, as it were, an inward draft blowing from the Gulf of California and the Pacific Ocean on the one hand, and from the Gulf of Mexico on the other, toward the continental center of low pressure." These winds are dried and heated by the land when they approach it, but once inland and encountering mountains, they rise and precipitate their moisture. The summer thunderstorms are fairly regular, and are equatorial in character since they come from the south. They produce their own kind of clouds, not those characteristic of the temperate zone. These clouds tower up from the horizon to a height of several thousand feet, white and dazzling, immense elongated cauliflowers with every part in convolution.

If it were not for the mountains, the whole of the

Southwest would be a desert. The winds from the two gulfs become so hot as they blow inland that, although they bear great quantities of water, they are still able to absorb whatever additional moisture they run across in stretches of desert already bone-dry from drought and sun. But the mountains force them to let go their burden. And fortunately, mountains have ways of impounding rain as well as snow and ice, and of sending the water down slowly enough to the lower lands for man to make the most of it.

Water does not always come down slowly from the mountains. A characteristic of mountain country, worse in the eroded Southwest than elsewhere, is the danger that follows heavy rainstorms at higher elevations. The run-off comes down the dry beds of previous torrents, called arroyos, sometimes without warning, at other times carrying boulders that grind one another with a low thunder that makes you prick up your ears. In places bridges cross these arroyos, but even the main highways generally dip for them. Signs on each bank warn the unaccustomed motorist, if it is a bad dip or arroyo. People used to the region rarely take chances. There is a spectacular dip near Bernalillo where the boulders from the Sandia mountains hit the concrete apron and bound over the roadway. Cars keep a respectful distance, but I have seen easterners wading across to get the depth of the water before the boulders have stopped bounding. Once at such an arroyo a flying rock hit a man on the head and killed him.

Mrs. William Skaggs operates a filling station at Valentine, Arizona. In a torrential rain not so long ago a California car pulled into her station for shelter. There is an arroyo in this little valley, and a few moments later a seven-foot flood came down it. The motorists heard it coming, sped from their car and got inside the station, but the water flooded the station, too. They had shut the door and could not open it, and were trapped inside. Rather than drown they broke a high window, so the newspaper account said, and led by the courageous Mrs. Skaggs all swam to safety through the raging torrent. Having seen these raging torrents, I have trouble visualizing their feat, but it is good that they escaped. They were fortunate. Even in desert country it pays to know how to swim.

There are too many tragedies. Recently a Mrs. Leddy and her five children left Globe, Arizona, to drive to Fort Bayard, N. M., to join Leddy, an employee of the Chino copper mines at Santa Rita. Their automobile was caught in a flash flood twenty miles south of Silver City on the Lordsburg highway. The water swirled through the sedan and drowned Mrs. Leddy, her ten-year-old daughter Betty, and her two sons, Owen and Everett, who were eighteen and fourteen years old. Two children escaped drowning, Vivian who is seven, and Clara, twelve. They spent the rest of the night in the wrecked car among their dead. At dawn they broke a window and crawled out, and were taken to Silver City by a passing motorist.

One summer day a WPA worker named Juan Martinez, his wife, and nine-year-old daughter Frances, were walking from El Rito to Abiquiu. They were resting in a dry arroyo when a five-foot wall of water came noiselessly upon them. It picked up all three and carried them downstream, but Martinez and his wife were able to escape. They lost their little girl. She was carried on down to the Chama river, and despite many searchers the remains of the child were not discovered for some days.

2. Weather

The Weather. The wind yesterday went through town at a fast burro trot; i.e. 5 m.p.h. It came from the S.E. going N.W. High temperature, 55 degrees at 3:00 P.M.; low 40 degrees at 11:30 P.M. Humidity 33—which is practically no humidity at all.
—*New Mexico Capital-Examiner*, Santa Fe

I DO NOT quote this charming weather report to prove anything. The April day in question may have been lovelier in other parts of the country. But the weather of the Southwest differs markedly from the weather elsewhere. You might call it more independent; there is a Southwest saying that only fools and tenderfeet predict the weather. People native to the piñon country who visit Chicago or New York in winter for the first time return quite surprised. "We had to buck terrible storms," said one old fellow after a month in Chicago. The Southwest is not free of storms, even bad ones, and dusters can be particularly trying; but in general and notably in summer because of the moist winds blowing inland from the two gulfs, climatic disturbance tends to be local and to make little autonomic demand.

Of the twenty-seven cyclone tracks across the United States as represented in the Van Cleef charts, only two cross New Mexico and Arizona. These two states are practically out of the path of the storms which lash the rest of the country except for southern California and the inland portion of the south. I can easily show what this exemption from strain means. As I write, the states to the north and northeast of us are experiencing a severe storm. It was first reported in my paper on Armistice Day, Monday. Tuesday the gale reached eighty miles an hour in Wisconsin, sixty-five in Chicago, and sixty-three in St. Louis. In the states through which it had passed, the Dakotas, Montana, and Wyoming, the temperature went below zero. Tornadic winds entered Louisiana, Arkansas, and Tennessee. On Thursday the temperature fell below frost as far south as Tallahassee and Jacksonville, New Orleans barely escaping with 34 degrees. Snow began again to fall in the northern areas; and on Friday, the fifth day of the storm, 4.8 inches fell in Chicago, a record for so early in the season. By the end of the week it was possible to count the number of dead. Thirty-seven seamen, most of them from the freighters *Davock* and *Minch,* lost their lives when the vessels foundered off Ludington, and there could hardly be hope for twenty-seven more, missing three days. On land, in Minnesota, Iowa, and Wisconsin, twenty-nine hunters died in the blizzard, and one hundred and four other persons perished in a dozen states from New York to Colorado.

This tragic storm affected New Mexico and Arizona only to the extent of making them unseasonably cold. Early Sunday morning, November 10, an unpredicted light snow suddenly fell. It was followed by a northwest wind which blew for four days, but never became a gale. On two successive nights the temperature in Santa Fe fell to nine above. By Thursday the weather was normal again. The Southwest thus had a taste of the storm before the rest of the country, which was unusual; generally the great cyclonic disturbances whip back at us several days later.

Almost always in summer, and often in winter, storms in the Southwest are entirely local. Here is a recent example. On March 3, 1940, the heaviest snow on record fell in Santa Fe. It was not predicted. It began about four o'clock on a Sunday afternoon without preliminaries. That Sunday morning had been calm and bright, but in the early afternoon wisps of clouds formed long streamers. My friend Gustave Baumann, who was going to supper at Los Alamos Ranch on the Pajarito Plateau thirty miles north of Santa Fe, threw his chains out of the car just before starting. Nobody, so far as I learned afterward, had put off any trips because the weather did not feel right. Southwesterners rarely take the weather into consideration, anyway.

They have the habit of going long distances to Sunday dinner, whether at noon or evening. Vegas people go to Raton or Santa Fe, Santa Fe people to Taos or Albuquerque or Belen, and think nothing of it. The inordinate distances have always been familiar, and the automobile makes them appear easy. Besides, though it may be raining or snowing where you live, the chances are it won't be where your friends live. Despite the increase in paved roads many people carry shovels still, towing ropes, extra blankets. You can always stay with your friends overnight, if you are caught in some unexpected way. It is not a land of tiny apartments and Murphy beds.

The storm which began in Santa Fe that Sunday afternoon lasted five hours and left behind it fourteen inches of wet snow. Its range was limited. Raton, one hundred and eighty-nine miles away, had no snow whatever. At Springer there were six inches, at Vegas ten, at Albuquerque and Gallup none, and none at Domingo, Cerrillos, Stanley, or Galisteo. But Espanola, twenty-five miles to the north, was buried, the roof of the dance hall caved in, and stranded motorists filled all the houses. At Taos there was only a flurry; at Tres Ritos the downfall was greater than anywhere else. It was fitting enough for Tres Ritos, because sixty enthusiastic skiers were in that mountain village for the second annual Taos ski meet.

Thus the storm extended less than two hundred

miles, making a path hardly thirty miles wide. The rest of the United States was undisturbed. The chainless Baumanns stayed overnight at Los Alamos Ranch, and barely made it to the top of the mesa at all. Other friends of ours, Ruth and Henry Alexander, were on their way home from dinner in Albuquerque and found no snow till within ten miles of Santa Fe. They had come to that point in an hour and a quarter, and spent the next two hours getting home from the outskirts of the town. In the foothills the snow lingered, and one elderly couple on a ranch did not come into town for four or five days. Their friends grew anxious and went out to the ranch with provisions. They found them completely out of food and down to "their last bottle of whiskey."

Weather is often unpredictable in mountain country out of the cyclonic tracks. Only once do I remember an alarming weather forecast in the years I have lived here. A little before Thanksgiving, 1931, the weather bureau notified people that a bad storm was coming down the Rockies from the Denver region and urged them sharply to "get all cattle and sheep off the ranges."

The cyclone is a mass of warmth and moisture that rotates counter-clockwise about a nucleus of low pressure. It travels at very high speed over the earth, pushed forward by a high pressure of polar air. Most of the great storms rush eastward in circumpolar fashion from the northwest coast or the Mackenzie Basin, and nearly all of them go out over the Atlantic by passing through New England. Their speed and magnitude, and the frequency of atmospheric change accompanying them, have an effect both for good and bad on the human organism. It is the moisture content of the air together with the frequency of these cyclones that constitutes a problem for the mechanisms in man that regulate temperature. The Puget Sound region is not frigid in any sense, but the rainfall (as heavy as in the valley of the Amazon) makes physiological chilling constant most of the year. The next great focal point of turbulence and demand upon the organism is Chicago and the Lakes, and the third and most severe point is New York and New England. Wyoming and Montana, being high and dry, escape much of the lashing. The region from southern California to Florida and Georgia, and the portions of the southern states not on the seacoast, escape practically all of it.

Dr. William F. Petersen in his work, *The Patient and the Weather,* compares the sections of the United States in the tracks of the cyclones with those comparatively free of them. He presents charts based on the draft statistics of adult young men in the World War, to show the distribution of cleft palate and other defects. That they center in the Northwest, the Lakes region, and New England, is curious, and gives interest to his remark that we are "resonators of environment, cosmic sounding boards." From his evidence that malformations are regionally distributed, Dr. Petersen proceeds to the theory that functional psychoses are regionally distributed also. "More people in certain regions become insane." The regions of intensity in his charts are again the paths of the great storms. He feels, too, that mental superiority, so far as his methods of analysis permit conclusions, must be "distinctly regional in its distribution; the region involved is that of the cyclonic tracks." Mental inferiority, conversely, is "regionally distributed in the meteorologically more stable sections of the country." He acknowledges that if the North produces more mentally superior persons per capita of the white population, the reason may lie in the educational handicaps of the South and Southwest, the relative poverty, infection with hookworm, an unbalanced diet, and so on. Yet granting these objections, he points out that there are fewer psychoses in the South. You would expect that a condition unfavorable for the development of mental superiority would produce a larger number of psychoses, but it is not so.

Admitting the difficulty of determining what mental superiority is, the doctor bases his charts on *American Men of Science,* particularly on the one thousand individuals in the book who are starred by their colleagues as achieving outstanding distinction. He resorts also to the college psychological examinations (1930), the draft material, *Who's Who,* and the *Cyclopedia of American History.* The evidence of the charts seems to support his contention that the mentally inferior, the mediocre, and those afflicted with normalcy, preponderate in the regions where cyclones trouble not. Genius, brightness, comeliness, on the other hand, and their counterparts, insanity, feeble-mindedness, physical malformation, seem to do better where the weather picks you up and stands you on your head every few weeks.

It is easy to imagine that people who live in New York and New England, say, where the population is dense, competition of every kind keen, climatic contrasts sharp and amounting to one blow after another with soothing kisses in between, might either go mad or wind up in *Who's Who.* Nor can the South and the Southwest ever hold up their end in a contest of this sort. The human organism is simply not flogged into extraordinary mental exertion, either in the easy-going South or the expansive and cordial Southwest. But the achievement of a sound and balanced living, and the appearance of the right leaders to show us the way, may not depend on stimulations like weather or overpopulation, both of which can resemble cup after cup of strong coffee. It may depend on something quite different, upon diet let us say. Diet is now being investigated as zealously as weather, and it may account

for our celebrities and our misfits to a greater extent
than we guess. All light from all angles is welcome, for
the problem is not simple. Or it may be found that
right living depends on something altogether different—on a kind of religious attitude, the way groups of
people value one another and value nature.

As time goes on the South and the Southwest will
become less appallingly ill-fed and illiterate. At present only South Carolina can surpass New Mexico in regard to illiteracy. If it comes to diet, surely there is
little good one can say about southern or Mexican
ways of cooking, to the extent that they are based on
the frying pan, "that man-destroying weapon," as
Langdon Mitchell called it. Later, it may be, these regions may offer their contribution to the American
search for what is worthwhile in living. On the other
hand, they may be offering this contribution today, in
spite of all their handicaps. The Indians and the Span-
ish-speaking people may be offering it. Their histories
reveal a most remarkable ability to live and multiply in
a discouraging land, and not always at the expense of
one another. And we do not look in *Who's Who* for a
great spiritual leader like Klah, the Navajo shaman.

The effect of altitude on the human being is beginning also to be investigated. Aeronautics has given im-
petus to researches on the effects of high altitude; but
moderate altitudes like 7,000 feet ought to make ascer-

tainable differences, also. A moderate altitude is rather widely considered good for the digestion. Nietzsche, who suffered from constipation, laments somewhere that he did not sooner leave the humid low-lying German cities for the invigorating Alps. Most people coming to the altitude of Santa Fe sleep hard and talk a great deal for the first four or five days. Others find difficulty getting to sleep, but do not mind it. Still others mind it, and become rather morose.

Yandell Henderson of Yale, in his remarkable *Adventures in Respiration*, tells of the scientific observations of his party of four (Haldane, Schneider, and Douglas were with him) during a residence on the top of Pike's Peak (14,100 feet). He says that during his stay on the peak, hundreds of people made the ascent, by rail, donkey, or foot. "They exhibited all degrees of mountain sickness from headache to fainting. But of all the symptoms, those involving the mind, particularly the judgment and temper, were most striking and often continued to develop for some hours even after a short stay at the summit and immediate descent. Indeed, the late Professor William Bayliss, after reading the account of the expedition in the *Philosophical Transactions of the Royal Society*, was fully justified in the remark that 'Perhaps all unreasonable people are suffering from lack of oxygen in their brains.' The observations of McFarland and his companions in the recent expedition to the Andes tend to the same conclusion."

Pike's Peak is of course twice as high as Santa Fe or Flagstaff or Taos, but I am struck by this paragraph on oxygen deficiency and human unreasonableness. For in the medium altitude of Santa Fe, when only moderately fatigued I am sometimes conscious of an irritability hard to account for. Others tell me they have a similar experience. Yet I do not remember hearing of it from people born or brought up here.

3. Piñones

New Mexico's piñon crop was estimated at approximately 6,000,000 pounds this fall, but with markets uncertain. . . .

—*Albuquerque*, New Mexico, *Tribune*

THE PIÑON tree is a disarming and perfect creation of nature's. I first touched and smelled it some twenty years ago, when my train was delayed for two hours on a February afternoon near Laguna Pueblo. I stepped down into the freshness and vastness of the diminutive forest and as I walked about among the blue-green odorous trees I felt like a giant, for over their heads was the horizon of the mountains. On a near-by hill was the ancient Indian town, the first pueblo I had ever seen. I was pleased that houses could be so unpretentious, built simply of the earth and leaving nothing to be improved upon. So with the little trees: they gave me the pleasure that comes of small perfect things which adapt their forces without scattering or waste. With the strength of their roots they plainly held the earth tight in its fight against erosion.

22

The piñon (Pinus edulis) is the most prominent characteristic of the Upper Sonoran life-zone, and does not occur outside it. So you encounter the piñon chiefly in New Mexico and northern Arizona, but also to some extent in southern Utah and Colorado, west Texas, and northern Mexico when you reach an elevation of five thousand feet and pass from the hot shadeless plains to the coolness of rolling slopes and sharp inclines on the northern side of which snow lingers. In among the trees the blue grama grass begins to grow; for miles in every direction the land is spick and span as a well-cared-for park. You ride horseback through the dwarf groves for hours finding no more clutter than the occasional woodcutter leaves. Near a native or Indian town, the piñones and their constant companions, the sabinas (junipers), will be harvested for firewood, but generally without endangering their future growth.

Three-quarters of New Mexico and a great part of northern Arizona are Upper Sonoran, and so piñones are widespread. But in these regions you can quickly ascend from the Upper Sonoran to the Transition zone (where there is fishing and hunting among the big pines), or descend to the Lower Sonoran, where the mesquite and creosote plants cling to life with their elaborate leaflessness. Above the Transition zone come the aspens of the Canadian belt, the tiny mountain flowers of the Hudsonian, and then the gaunt summits

of the Arctic-Alpine. These states have all varieties of
climate, tree life, bird life; what is true in one place is
false in another. You can watch apricot trees blossom
day after day if you follow them up different grada-
tions of climate.

It is in the piñon country near river valleys or
springs that man has for centuries done best with his
life. For piñon country is grazing country. In and
through the trees go the flocks of sheep and goats,
from the western boundary of the Navajo reservation
to Raton and its mesas on the East. Neither piñon nor
sabina will ever create a generation of lumber million-
aires. There is no money in them, and they will stay
to carpet hundreds of miles with their green. Sabina
wood is impossible for open fireplaces because it snaps
and throws sparks, but it makes a quick and lasting
heat for cooking, and keeps flues free of soot. The
sabina takes a long time to rot, and so is good for
fence posts. If I use the expression "U. S. American"
for people coming to New Mexico and Arizona from
the other states, it is only to avoid the common usage
that refers to them, whether they are Jewish, German,
Irish, Yankee or Greek, as "Americans," "Nordics," or
"Anglos."

The piñon nut (called also the pine nut and the Indian nut) has always been an important food to Indians and natives. They harvest only a small fraction
of the crop, for piñones stretch mile after mile, and

the demand is less than the supply. In good years the crop may be worth a million dollars, and the pickers get perhaps a third of this amount. About four-fifths of the crop is sold outside the state, most of it going to the east side of New York. There the pushcart vendors sell the nuts to people who miss the Russian pine nuts and the Italian pistachios of their homelands. The piñon is a good nut, quite small, higher in protein and carbohydrates than pecans, but lower in fat. It keeps well; if unshelled it can go a year without turning rancid.

Every year there are piñon nuts to gather. But the heavy crop comes every third, fifth, or seventh year, according to what you like to think. The nuts require two years to mature; drought shrivels them. To gather them is an occasion for the whole family to work together, and if relatives are visiting, to get some work out of the relatives. Cars and wagons lie like beetles along the highways and byways. You hear people and children chattering not far away, with as much noise as the piñon-jays whose blue wings flash among the branches. The dwarf trees are suddenly a vineyard; the barren land turns fruitful and calls for pickers. Little children run from tree to tree picking up the nuts that have fallen. Sometimes they find the cache of a squirrel and get ten or fifteen pounds at a stroke. Against the dark green of the tree the cones are a beautiful henna inside and flare out in ever wider clusters of dark little coffee berries, until they literally bend backward. The taste is pine and sunshine and popcorn, and peanuts too in a way. Grown-up people spread a sheet underneath the tree and beat the nuts down with an old broom. They take along stout flour-sacks, and when they return to town in the October dusk after a long day and two meals in the open, the sacks are full, and they have made sure of one source of food for the winter.

The country is at its best when the piñons ripen. The Upper Sonoran ranges are comparatively free of pests at any season, but you have to look out for the red ants, which sting diabolically, and for the little black-tailed rattler (not the diamond-back, he lives in the Lower Sonoran). By October snakes and ants have gone. The ground is warm, the little trees make everything cosy; you can lie down anywhere and take a nap. It is a kind of Garden of Eden.

Even U. S. Americans become expert in cracking the shells with their teeth. But it takes an old Indian or native to show what can be done. Piñons go in one corner of the mouth and the shells come out the other. Sitting against a warm wall in the winter sun, people can keep it up for hours. Political speakers grow used to the cracking and munching of their audiences. After the broadcasts of the world series in the plazas of many towns, the pavements close to the curbs are deep with shells, and tires of cars make a noise like tearing cloth. At the public and parochial schools the janitors begin to hate the young human squirrels who leave such a litter in their desks.

The piñon crop, being a free gift of God and an occasion for families to go into the country together in the perfect weather (for October in the Southwest is a dream), fills thousands of people with memories that make life good and worth living, not just endurable. It is a special and dear experience.

Occasionally some visitor is repelled by the piñon landscape. I remember Stanley Vestal's saying of the landscape between Santa Fe and Tesuque, "those strangely depraved hills studded with stunted piñon, hills pink and salmon in color, dead hills or dead alive, looking like hams stuck with cloves." His remark is as accurate as it is vivid about places where erosion is at work. But in those very places the dwarf trees are doing their greatest favor to man; they are keeping the hills from slipping away.

In a country where the winds keep pushing and often bear sand or snow or rain, all elevated shapes tend to become pyramids sooner or later, cones of earth that look like triangles reaching their apexes to the sky. The little trees cling desperately to these cones, and only give up when the battle is lost. From the mesas which they forest thickly you see them thin out as they approach a stretch of badly eroded lands, from thousands to hundreds, then to dozens. When the white lightning forks into these towers and tombs of erosion, or a sunspot plays on them, you see revealed a few dark spots that are trees fighting for their life and for the earth's life.

These scenes have been the same for ages. So it is odd to read in the paper that old-timers are to hold a banquet, with tall tales of cowboy and trail days; that the cowboy poet will be there and sing ballads; that the widow of the hero of a famous Indian fight is to talk.

Such people would, of course, be old-timers in a sense the country east of the Mississippi would not know about, for that country can no longer recall its frontier days. Still, they are not old-timers here in the sense that the Spanish Americans are, whose people go back three centuries, or the Navajo and the Apache, who go back to 1200 at least, or the Pueblo Indians who are immemorial. The stubborn continuance of these other groups foreshortens in our view the old-timer who had his day only a couple of generations since, when the pony express came over the Santa Fe trail. A Southwest newspaper is like the surface of a lake, and all the fish in the lake from the beginning of time to the minnows dumped into it yesterday, have a way of coming to the surface, or of floating along near it so you can see them.

Our American landscape has two major themes—

forests and grass plains. The Southwest entwines the
two strangely and memorably, by turning plains into
deserts, and forest trees into bushes. The stories of the
men who explored the virgin lands east of the Mississippi are not like the stories of Southwest exploration.
The landscape of piñones remains as it always was, for
man is not able to change mountains and mesas; and
although he can change semi-arid regions to an extent,
it is only to an extent, and one that may not last. But
the characteristic of the virgin lands in the East was
the great forest. We cannot visualize today the white
man's early days there, for the forest has gone. With
its going the streams have changed that carried the
voyageurs and the explorers. The animals they lived
upon, and the tribes of Indians they mingled with or
fought with, have also disappeared. It has all changed.
Patches of tall evergreens remain in the protection of
hills or mountains, and remnants of the delicate hard-
wood forests in the woodlot of farms. They suggest
something of what the land was in its entirety and the
abundant life of the first inhabitants, in the vast damp
shade and the occasional spaces of sun. There were no
vistas in the East in the sense that the piñon country
is full of vistas. That very early eastern life as it came
westward down the rivers seems night-covered, half-
blind, unrestrained, licentious, cruel. On the other
hand, the early life of the Southwest was much as it is
today, sun-filled and wide-eyed, yet trembling with

mirage and shifts of altitude; cautious, yet unworldly and visionary.

The early East must have been a remarkable and beautiful scene of physical life. There was interconnection and interdependence of man and the birds and animals, of streams, grasses, bushes, and forests, with everything dependent on the forest humus. But when the ax felled the first tree, when the Indian drank his first bottle of whiskey, the whole fabric of existence began to unravel and nothing could be done about it. In the piñon country what interdependence there is centers about the water supply; there is no lack of physical life, only one grows less aware of it than of distance, dearth, death, timelessness. Call the Southwest a spiritual experience or not, it has forced people to face the realities of existence. This is noticeable not only in the Indian, though he has felt the regional influences longest. It comes out in the first Europeans who ever entered the region.

4. Núñez

In his new book *The Route of Cabeza de Vaca,* Cleve Hallenbeck proves that the explorer and his companions entered what is now New Mexico and Arizona. They first followed the Colorado River, then the Pecos River from a point near Pecos, Texas, to Carlsbad, New Mexico, then went northwest to the slopes of the Sacramento-Guadalupe Mountains, circling those ranges and proceeding south to the vicinity of El Paso, and thence following the Rio Grande up to Rincon; from there they went southerly through the corner of Arizona into Sonora. . . .
— *Roswell,* New Mexico, *Daily Record*

A THEORY about the exact route a man followed four centuries ago is still news in New Mexico and Arizona papers; the sky and the horizon are still the same long room the man trudged through. In a hard land, routes are of consuming interest. Besides, the Southwest preserves its history as the tombs of the Kings preserved the royal mummies of Egypt; only, in the Southwest nothing seems mummified. Ideas from each period of the past mingle with the ideas of today.

There can be little doubt that Núñez Cabeza de Vaca and his three companions were the first Europeans to enter the American Southwest. It is plain too that they entered the piñon country, for Núñez gives us our first description of the little tree. It was a good season for piñon nuts, and he credits them with saving the lives of the party after their starvation on the Texas plains.

Núñez was the lieutenant of Pamfilo de Narváez in the exploring expedition which sailed from Spain in 1527. The members of the expedition who survived the hardships of Florida were lost in the Gulf of Mexico, with the exception of these four men. They managed to reach the mainland, perhaps where Galveston now stands, and struck inland. The story is extraordinary. Núñez was a man who liked people and felt for them, all kinds of people, rich and poor, young and old, sick and healthy. He was a discoverer against his will and no conqueror, and came along destitute and lost in the course of this journey during which he tasted what must be the strongest drink known—the belief of the people he met that he was a savior and healer, a way out of their human troubles. His three companions were Castillo and Dorantes, fellow Spaniards, and a slave of Dorantes', the Arab Negro Estevanico. When shipwrecked the Spaniards were between thirty-five and forty, the Negro younger. The wanderers were lost in the wilds from 1528 to 1536, and day after day kept on toward the setting sun, until they entered Sonora and there encountered fellow Spaniards. They had lost their clothes when a raft upset on the coast of Texas and so these first whites to cross the continent crossed it naked as savages. After he had reached Mexico City, taken a good rest, and cut off his long beard, Núñez set down his experiences for the benefit of the Emperor Charles V. The first written account of the Southwest contains the themes of the entire history of the peoples of that region: exile, hardship, adaptation, and hope.

They came to villages where many had an eye clouded, and some were totally blind. In other villages the natives were so anxious to receive their blessing that the travelers fainted of exhaustion from the bestowing of it. In still others, the poor folk, their bodies deformed, starved, wasted, so insisted on touching them all over that it took three and four hours to get through with the suppliants. Some of these natives ate only powdered straw for part of the year. In parts of the journey the Spaniards were attended by three or four thousand Indians, who had heard of their cures. Núñez says it went past human endurance to make the sign of the cross over every morsel the Indians ate.

After such experiences it was shocking to the party that when at last they fell in with fellow Spaniards in Sonora, their countrymen should turn out to be slave-catchers, and should actually try to enslave the Indians who had been following them. An altercation ensued. One Spaniard made a speech, telling the Indians that Núñez and his friends were only in a fashion Christians, had lost their way, and were people with no luck; while they, the Spaniards on horseback, were the real Christians and the lords of the land, to be obeyed and served. The Indians, being fairly bright, responded that the real Christians apparently lied, Núñez and his friends could not possibly be Christians. Núñez cured the sick, while the caballeros killed even the healthy. Núñez went naked and barefoot, while the caballeros wore clothes, and rode horseback, and stuck people with lances and dragged them along in chains. Núñez asked for nothing and gave away all he was given, while the caballeros never gave anybody anything and had no other aim than to steal.

People wonder how these four men were able to survive experiences that proved too terrible for the other 572 members of the Narváez expedition. And then how they continued to withstand the hardships of landscape and climate for seven more years. But the reasons for endurance are questions that underlie many happenings in the Southwest. No doubt suffering was not utterly hateful to Núñez and his companions; it must have resulted in certain ideas or feelings which kept them going. Perhaps they found it easier to do the suffering themselves than to make others suffer. The man who is cruel is also willful, perhaps, and when disaster comes he is apt to succumb to it, while there is never any guarantee that the meek will succumb. In Florida the quartette survived swamps,

snakes, Indians, mosquitoes, despair; on the sea the
blistering sun, the lack of fresh water, and despair; on
the mainland enslavement, hunger, the freezing winds
of winter, the appalling sun of summer, and despair.
They could take unlimited punishment because they
could adapt themselves to practically anything. To
adapt yourself, perhaps you have to submit, have to
stop thinking that you amount to much or that you can
enforce your will on other people, and on the earth.
These men may have stopped being Europeans and
become something like Indians. I don't know. There is
a passage early in the story when Núñez admits he sat
down and cried over his troubles. Some Indians came
along, and he was such a pitiful sight that they sat
down beside him and cried, too. No doubt the discov-
ery Núñez made was that people are human beings.

That he treated them so we have later testimony in
the history of the Coronado expedition. Castañeda,
writing of the return of the army detachment from
west Texas under Maldonado, says, "Núñez had passed
through this place, so that the natives presented Don
Rodrigo with a pile of tanned skins and other things,
and a tent as big as a house . . . but the soldiers were
afraid the gifts would not be divided evenly. . . . In
less than a quarter of an hour nothing was left but the
empty ground. . . . The women and some others
were left crying, because they had thought that the
strangers were not going to take anything, but would

bless them as Núñez and Dorantes had done when they passed through here."

Everyone admires Núñez, but there is skepticism about his tales of healing Indians. Yet people who see others as human beings can do strange things to help them. Núñez thought about Indians as fellow sufferers, and was excited when it was forced on his attention that he had it in his power to heal them. It is quite plain in his book. Love and hope are sentiments that inspire many people to good deeds, and it is clear they make possible a welcoming attitude toward new ideas about life. The truth is, I imagine, that Núñez through really caring about the luckless Indians practiced an intensified form of religion the race will know more about in the future. His adventure was a breathtaking sweep into the everlasting good.

The question of how one should act toward Indians was a torment to Imperial Spain, and probably the most vexing of the social questions precipitated by its period of sudden colonial expansion. In 1550 the Emperor Charles V called a conference, or public hearing, at Valladolid to determine whether the conquest of the Americas was just. The antagonistic points of view were presented by Las Casas and Sepúlveda, and both men based their arguments on passages in Aristotle. One October day, out in the autumn cottonwoods of the Tesuque valley, Lewis Hanke of the Library of Congress told me that he had examined the records of the conference, and the remarks of Las Casas alone ran to 550 folio pages. It is small wonder that the hearings lasted a full year. Hanke's study of sixteenth-century Spanish Indian policy, *The First Social Experiments in America,* is as absorbing as it is terse.

Sepúlveda held that men are divided into two classes, the masters and the slaves. The slaves express themselves through the masters, and cannot be held to have souls. In this fashion the enslavement of the Indian populations seemed right and natural. But Las Casas proved a stubborn opponent. The cards were stacked against him, for Peru and Mexico had already been conquered, with their immense wealth, and the ruling class could not be expected to forego the results of their great and hazardous initial investment in the expeditions. But Las Casas, in his 550 pages of remarks, held tight to the doctrine that all men, white, black, or copper-colored, have souls. The hearing came to no conclusion; everyone was worn out by its length and learning. Although Sepúlveda's ideas were congenial to the nobility and expedient to the hour, amounting to saying that God's blessings were on the conquests and by all means let them proceed, he could not win the decision. The conquests did go on, of course, but with many indications that Spain was uneasy about them. A territory so unprofitable as New

Mexico would never have been maintained, for example, if the Crown (with the buzzing of the Dominicans about it) had not taken seriously the idea that Indians have souls. New Mexico came to be a missionary outpost maintained so that the padres could convert the Pueblo Indians.

5. Estevanico

The few people who stopped in at the Pueblo of Santo Domingo yesterday had the good luck to see the comparatively rare dance in which the Indians make fun of their conquerors. Dancers imitating Americans kept looking at their watches anxiously . . . the Spanish conquistadores rode hobby horses and were very haughty. They had with them the famous Negro Estevanico, who made leering faces at all the women. . . .

—*The Santa Fe New Mexican*

ESTEVANICO, Dorantes' Moorish slave, was no healer, but he had a soul like everybody else, if Las Casas is right in saying that people have souls. The soul of little Steven veered constantly in the direction of having a good time; and since joy is not to be discounted, I am glad the Arab Negro from Azamor has as much right in our earliest Pantheon as Coronado or Núñez himself. We can think of him as the prototype of people nowadays who come to the Southwest, whether to reside or to vacation, to escape what they find enslaving in the conventions or competition of the industrial East.

The appearance of Núñez and his companions in

Mexico City caused a sensation. From what we know
of them, these were not men to fabricate stories of
treasure and of golden cities. But the immense rev-
enues of the Aztecs and the Incas added to the crown
by Cortés and Pizarro led adventurous men into disas-
trous dreaming. People were ready to hear tales of
treasure, were ready to believe they had heard tales
of treasure, even when they had not.

The Arab Negro talked a great deal, both drunk and
sober. Dorantes could not have thought of him still as
a slave after their eight years together, but it is plain
that he could not give him his freedom. The Negro
had grown too valuable because of what he had gone
through. Mendoza, the viceroy, tried to persuade Dorantes to head an exploring expedition north, but
Dorantes had had enough exploring. He turned Estevan over to Mendoza, or else the latter bought the
slave from him. The viceroy was not a credulous man,
and he wished to investigate with only a small outlay
of money the possibilities of treasure to the north.

In Mexico City lived a Franciscan, Marcos of Niza
(Nice), who had been in Peru, and was a man of endurance and ability. It occurred to the viceroy to send
Niza and Estevanico forth, to reconnoiter the north
country. Estevan could guide the priest, and the priest
could obtain facts about the land, the souls to be
saved, and the riches available. If a bonanza were discovered, the priest would return with the news and not

claim the country for himself, as a soldier might do. But the viceroy wished to check the accuracy of the priest further, and for this purpose, after Marcos had started, he dispatched a man named Melchior Díaz on an independent investigation. No one in the colonial history of Mexico bears a reputation for such iciness of judgment as this Díaz.

The Negro contrived to leave his companion a day or so behind. They kept in touch by messenger, but once separated, the friar never laid eyes on him again. Estevanico was a slave, and still a slave after the eight years' journey during which he had been as free a man as his companions and no doubt the life of the party. He becomes a symbolic figure as one pictures him, with the church on his heels looking for souls to be saved, while behind the friar, waiting for his report about treasure, were the viceroy and the dogs of conquest. What Estevan symbolizes, if you like, is the life of the ordinary man since history began, enslaved by government, pursued by religion, trying to snatch some moments of pleasure on his march to the grave. The situation was clear to Estevan; he had only a short time of liberty, and had better make the most of it. As it turned out, only seventy-three days of his life remained when he started north.

A good deal of later history hinges on the psychology of this Negro. If he had gone along dutifully with Niza, the pair would no doubt have been allowed to enter the villages of the Pueblo Indians and would have seen their naked poverty. In that event Spain would never have tackled the destitute north in the extravagant fashion of an armed expedition.

Later writers make interesting vignettes of Estevanico's journey, for all the hearsay is of a kind to kindle the carnal imagination of writers. He had the African's flair for making an impression, and for elaborate make-believe. As he passed through the land of the Pimas and the Ópatas (what is now southern Arizona), he carried a gourd decorated with bells and feathers, such as medicine men might use, and it brought him great respect. These Indians are polygamous, and we are assured that he was never without maidens who appealed to him. Men followed him, too, from these good-natured and easy-going villages, made his camp at night, and procured his food, so that Estevan had nothing to do but enjoy life. But he could not linger to enjoy it, for the priest was hurrying along behind him. I hope that the tales are true, that even if it was mock heroics, Estevanico had his day of glory, his harem, his slaves. As he proceeded with his entourage across the plateaus of giant yucca and branching cacti in northern Mexico, he achieved an unforgettable variation on the business of being a conqueror.

Having come over into New Mexico, he approached the first village of the Zuñi Indians, who are part of the well-nigh indestructible culture of the Pueblos. These

Indians, unlike the indolent Pimas, are sober and in-
dustrious, good burghers like the Chinese, skilled in
preserving from marauders their women and their har-
vests. Estevanico sent on ahead his gourd and rattles.
When the old men (the rulers of the village) saw the
rattles, they threw them on the ground and stamped
on them, saying they knew what kind of people had
sent them, and those people had better stay away if
they valued their lives. Estevanico, undaunted, proceeded to the village, and was killed. A Zuñi legend
says that the old men "gave him a powerful kick,
which sped him through the air back to the south,
whence he came." But what the Zuñis told Coronado
the following year (1540), the general reported to
Mendoza, "They killed him because he assaulted their
women, whom the Indians love better than themselves." Probably he chucked a few girls under the
chin, or passed his arm round their waists, and thought
nothing of it, being a man with a harem. But it is better not to chuck Pueblo girls under the chin. Beyond
doubt the Zuñi were affronted by the free ways of this
"black Mexican." Estevan in his wanderings had not
encountered Indians of complicated psychology. His
failure to size up the Pueblos is understandable, for no
one can size them up.

Several days later Friar Marcos, horrified, gazed at
the pueblo from a neighboring hilltop. He must have

seen it gilded by the sunlight, for on his return to Mexico he described it as a golden city. It gave the Spaniards at the capital a fever. And Díaz of the icy judgment failed to return and report the truth until it was too late.

6. Coronado

The 400th anniversary of the coming of Coronado was officially recognized here tonight. The first of a series of Entradas [Coronado's entrance] was re-enacted in a play with a cast of 800. . . . The Spanish Ambassador to the United States, Juan F. de Cardenas, was a guest of honor. . . .

Highlight of the opening of the centennial, was a speech by Pablo Abeyta, governor of Isleta Pueblo and president of the All-Pueblo Indian Council, who said, "I do not agree with all this talk about Coronado. I don't know what they mean by Spanish culture . . . the Spanish got lost on the ocean and accidentally ran across this continent. They thanked God for giving it to them, and stuck their flag into it. They never asked the Indians how they felt about it."

Abeyta, a graduate of St. Michael's College in Santa Fe, insisted that Coronado had come to New Mexico with war, while the Indians wanted only peace. . . .

—Albuquerque, New Mexico, *Journal*

THE SPANISH ambassador had a good laugh, I am told, at the outspoken Abeyta. It amuses one that Abeyta should still be orating about the wrongs done his people four centuries ago, when long since the conquerors have in turn been conquered, and now people of every description are living in the Southwest together and trying to make a go of it in common.

All that Señor Cárdenas as an official of the Franco regime would have in common with Coronado was Spanish blood. Coronado was an extraordinarily rare type of man, not disclosing the motivation of his life to a casual glance, whether the glance be a Pueblo Indian's, a Franco Spaniard's, or a U. S. American's. This is the only instance in the history of the Southwest, and one of very few instances in the history of the whole country, that we can see a true aristocrat.

The ruling class of a great empire is brought up to serve certain ideals. It does not grow freely and naturally; it is pulled this way and that, cut and trimmed in a hundred special ways, to meet the exigencies of its tradition. The traditions of a class embody its savoir faire, and the ruling class has to be guided by these traditions even when they run counter to the selfish desires of the individual. The aristocrat belongs to a relatively small group privileged to rule by their patrician birth, and trained from infancy to share the sympathies, habits, and temper of mind common to their equals.

We can make out that Coronado was an aristocrat to whom aristocracy was an almost sacred calling. It is fully as rare as to find a democrat who takes seriously, not the vague idea of government by the people, for anybody can take a vague idea seriously, but the practice of social equality and sharing in daily life. But I find a democrat of this kind in a recently published account by John Maloney, an official of the Red Cross, of his visit to Finland at the time the Karelian Isthmus was ceded to Russia. He attended a meeting of business men called by President Kallio to discuss the care of the évacués. The Finnish government was spending two million dollars monthly for its homeless citizens, and the responsibility might last indefinitely. The business men discussed possible solutions for the problem facing a totally exhausted country. An exporter of wood and pulp, named Ake Gartz, had the answer.

To Ake Gartz the question involved went far beyond taxes, even though every Finn would have to have his taxes raised three or four hundred per cent. The great necessity was to find what would restore the spirit of the country. The families who had moved out of the ceded isthmus had made plain their faith in their little republic, and so the rest of the country must not let them down. Ake Gartz said he was sure every Finn would share what he had to safeguard these people, to give them land and new homes.

Here we have a democrat to whom democracy is a reality, and so Ake Gartz is an excellent contrast to our Spanish grandee. He appealed to his equals by invoking only the idea of what would be the right, friendly, human thing to do under the circumstances. He acted as an individual united to his fellows and his native land by ideas all understood and accepted. He did not speak as a member of a ruling class, in obedience to or to perpetuate a caste system.

When we first see Coronado in November, 1535, arriving in Mexico with the new viceroy, Antonio de Mendoza, he was already seasoned, a somebody from Salamanca, twenty-five years old, the second of four brothers (the third brother, Juan, was to be first mayor-general of Costa Rica). These four brothers were the sons of a Vasquez de Coronado, Lord of Coquilla and of the Tower of Juan Vasquez in Salamanca, and of his lady, Doña Isabel de Lujan. A family apparently influential and powerful, whether rich or not; in any event, a home where growing boys could learn dignity, decorum, how to speak, how to bow, how to use a rapier. How also to endure the restraints of a complicated and settled culture—the madness of avarice, of long evenings in the leather armchairs playing dominoes, of an existence lived in relation to the family and the clock.

So Coronado came to the New World, the friend of the viceroy, dependable ("one hundred per cent"), a young man to be counted on to stick, to stand by. The viceroy could have no fear of being double-crossed, of a dangerous *personal* ambition in his friend. Coronado's ambition was impersonal, to serve God, Emperor, viceroy; he was a most favorable example of a ruling aristocracy. So he was a young man who deserved to be well treated, to be married to an heiress, to be given land, to be a pillar of the viceregal court. These matters were speedily attended to. His bride was Beatriz de Estrada, daughter of the late royal treasurer. They made a good marriage, loyal to state and church, and proceeded to have children. The entry in the minutes of the town council of Mexico City, June 14, 1538, discloses that Coronado, barely three years in the land, was sworn in as an alderman, "married and with children." His mother-in-law had written to the King some years before complaining that in Mexico she could discover no suitable husbands for her daughters. She was happy with this paragon of a Coronado, gave him a lucrative and enormous ranch, gave him, too, her big house in the city, and behind it built a humbler one for herself.

Mendoza appointed the young man inspector for silver mines. At Amatepeque the Negro slaves had revolted and set up a black king of their own. Coronado had been sharpened for the use of the state; let him quell this revolt. He quelled it; he hanged and quartered twenty-five blacks. Mendoza appointed him his "meastresala," that is, his personal equerry and master of ceremonies. It required a special kind of man with everything the word grandee implies. A man of savoir and finesse as Spain understood those terms at the time of her greatness. A swordsman, a man who could be glacial, so that even the younger brother of a duke would hesitate to turn a witticism against him.

Above all, an exemplar. That most of all, a model for all the other young nobles in Mexico, the kind of personal life, the kind of demeanor, the viceroy searched for and was prepared to honor. For as many of the young men as possible must be sharpened for the use of God and Emperor, through the viceroy. It is the only way in which a great empire can continue to be great.

A democracy cannot train and reward its young hopefuls as group government does, whether the group be the patricians round a monarch or the advisers of a dictator. Democracy cannot function that way. It is an inward adventure, and its rewards are inward. As Montaigne said, the Monarch is within. " 'Tis a rugged road, to follow a pace so rambling and uncertain as that of the soul—to choose and lay hold of so many little nimble notions, 'tis a new and extraordinary undertaking."

And then the northern enterprise, which Mendoza had fears of and an instinct against, began to take shape as inevitable. Mendoza did not swallow the rumors of cities of gold. But the enterprise had to be, as it turned out; and he had the man to undertake it, Coronado. It was a problematical venture from any point of view, and the chief requisite was a man as leader who could command two hundred wild young bluebloods, keep his distance and their respect; mold them into useful beings; give them the day-by-day picture of the Spanish noble, daring, resourceful, God-fearing, courageous, humane, but when need be cruel.

What happened to the expedition, what it accomplished the world knows. But a detail of which only the student of human motive can see the significance is that Coronado encountered the returning Melchior Díaz before he had marched far, and learned from him the frigid truth, that there was nothing to the dream, there were no gold cities ahead, only hardship and thirst and hunger. Coronado and his staff talked the news over, but they kept it from the soldiers. Coronado decided to go ahead. He was trained to be selfless, and had no choice. He had been ordered to explore the north, and he explored it. He did the job Mendoza sent him out to do, did it thoroughly, did it amazingly.

We have certain glimpses of Coronado in his letters to Mendoza, and in the pages of Castañeda. At Zuñi he sees the adobe houses, the sharing of the water, the pottery making, the dances in the plaza, the natives in all aspects of their communal life. Does he really see them? Unfortunately he is not a reflecting individual, he is blinded by caste and class. He writes the viceroy that the natives seem of ordinary size and intelligent, yet lack the intelligence they ought to possess to build such houses ("for most of them go naked except for the loin cloth"). He was shrewder when it came to corn. He praises their corn-cakes ("the best I have ever seen anywhere") and their way of grinding corn ("one of these women will grind as much as four Mexicans"). But it was as close as he ever got to the secret life of the Pueblo Indian, this passing recognition that they had a way with the corn.

Because of the massacre at Tiguex the Pueblo Indians have a special detestation for Coronado. As Pablo Abeyta's words show, it still looms large in their minds as the symbol of Spanish oppression. It was a bad enough business, but it was less the responsibility of Coronado than of a lieutenant of his, who incidentally bore the same name as the Spanish ambassador, Cárdenas. Cárdenas was punished severely for it when he returned to Mexico, by exile and a heavy fine. As the long debate at Valladolid had shown, most Spaniards suspected that Indians had souls. The fear that it might be so could not be gainsaid so long as a single Dominican remained articulate.

The massacre itself (like the riot at Gallup long afterwards, which we shall come to in the industrial age) was an incident that might easily have been avoided. The weather near the present Bernalillo was very cold, and the Spaniards were shivering. They had long since thrown away the unsuitable armor in which they started out, and were wearing the cotton garments they found at Zuñi. They proposed to obtain heavier clothing from the twelve near-by pueblos and in a seemly manner. But the Indians were too dignified and too slow, and the impatient Spaniards stripped them, even the old men, of their blankets and cloaks. To retaliate, the Indians drove many of the horses to their villages. They barred the palisades and chased the beasts round and round "as in a bullfight," shooting them with arrows. "He who strikes first admits his ideas have given out," say the Chinese; and the Spaniards, beside themselves with fury, went berserk. They took sixty captives, and Cárdenas ordered stakes to be prepared. When the soldiers began to roast the first of them, the remainder fought for their lives and broke away. The land was level and they had no chance; mounted Spaniards rode them down one by one. The news spread that the newcomers did not abide by their peace terms, and never after did the Pueblo Indians really trust them. In every conquest the moment comes when resentment flares up in the conquered. Then the conqueror says, "We will teach him to be afraid of us." This completes the logic of force. So we cannot estimate at its true worth Coronado's general high excellence of character, for we incline today to judge a man by his attitude towards defenseless people.

The rest of Coronado's story is strange but pertinent, I believe, to the idea that the Southwest can be a psychological and personal experience. It is only within a very few years that the researches of scholars have revealed the general's later life. Something happened to him in the north country which sent him back to Mexico a changed man, no longer the model aristocrat. Núñez had been able to reconcile his traditions with the new world, the wilderness, he found himself in. Coronado failed to do so.

It was not the disappointment of finding no golden cities, for he had known before he left Mexico that that hope was doomed. He accomplished the giant's march into Kansas and came back to Tiguex in autumn in good time to prepare the army for winter. Castañeda, the historian of the expedition, says he planned to lead the whole army into the prairies the next spring. Then, while racing with Captain Maldonado, as he frequently did for amusement, Coronado fell off his horse. "His girth broke during the race and he fell over on the side where Don Rodrigo was, and as his horse passed over him it hit his head with its hoof."

While recovering from this accident, Coronado changed his mind about entering the prairies again. To return to Mexico as soon as possible he resorted to unworthy intrigue and stratagem. Castañeda also tells us that while he was ill, the general "recollected what a scientific friend of his in Salamanca had told him, that he would become a powerful lord in distant lands, and that he would have a fall from which he would never recover."

This prophecy remembered at such a time, preyed on Coronado. His action in the case of the soldier Truxillo on the journey north, had been sensible and healthy. This Truxillo, while swimming in a stream near Culiacan, had a vision; he saw himself kill Coronado, then marry the general's young widow and inherit all his goods. Niza preached a sermon about it, and there was so much talk among the soldiers that Coronado told Truxillo's captain to leave him behind. Most leaders would have done the same. For whether he dreamt the dream or not, Truxillo was a fool to relate it, or else he wanted to be left behind. In either case he was useless.

In 1542 Coronado returned to his governorship over New Galicia. We hear of him standing trial in an investigation of his rule by an official from Spain, one Tejada. The thirty-three charges against him included general neglect of duty, favoritism, irregularities of conduct, short accounts, setting a bad example by openly dicing and gambling, the acceptance of bribes, the cruel treatment of Indians (men, women, and children) on his ranches and in his mines. These are not the actions of a paragon, a true grandee. Coronado now seems a man in a daze, suddenly indifferent and heedless.

The general denied the charges brought against him,

but he made admissions so damaging that it amounted to guilt and he was fined 600 gold pesos. He lost his governorship. He appealed to the Council of the Indies, but nothing was done about it. He spent more and more time in Mexico City, oddly enough in his small duties as alderman. He attended to these duties so assiduously that he probably hoped to regain his reputation through them. His actions are still those of a man in a daze, but he is now clutching at a straw. He has no perspective, but he has fear. In 1548, when Coronado applied to the King for an office, Mendoza advised the court explicitly that he no longer considered him qualified for the service of government. The viceroy was aware of a change in his old friend so devastating there was no way to gloss it over.

Paul A. Jones, who has made accessible much of this new information about Coronado, inquires as to the general's incessant activities as an alderman, "Was it that he had at last found a position that suited his capabilities?" But the sneer is unfair. Coronado was a good soldier, who accomplished the task given him even though he knew from the beginning it could only mean defeat. And then we see him as a man to whom a doom came, no more like his former self than the moon is like the sun.

What Castañeda means by the "scientific" friend of Coronado's in Salamanca, who foretold the disaster, is not clear. The word "scientist" was then often applied to alchemists, as it still is to horologers and numerologists. The medieval alchemist could be an excellent judge of character, and had his own practical knowledge of psychology. Too many egocentric interests breed danger for anybody, and this danger has always been pretty well charted. Coronado as a youth could appear to some shrewd person too much of a paragon to maintain indefinitely the equilibrium of existence in a world that prefers the plastic to the rigid. In the Southwest a newcomer does not need to have a horse kick him on the head, to become different. But when a person is due to swing from one extreme to another, almost any form of accident can cause the change.

7. Pueblo Indians

Yesterday pagan rites of the Pueblos and ceremonials of Catholic Christianity mingled in the baptism of a Jemez Village baby named Green Mountain. . . . Father Raphael Weisenbach, Franciscan missionary priest at Jemez for twelve years, sprinkled holy water over the Jemez child from an Indian-made cup. Among the best students of southwestern Indians are missionary Catholic priests who live among their spiritual charges. They look kindly on most Indian rituals held over from a pre-Christian age, and turn them into Christian celebrations. . . .

The baptism at the church over, the Indians had their turn. Juan Celo the acting godfather, and Mary Reid the godmother, stood at the bed's edge while the family and neighbors gathered behind. Juan chanted in his native tongue—"May this baby not be blind." "No," answered his audience. "May this baby not be lame." "No," replied the others in unison . . . and so through a long prayer. At the end the godfather held an ear of corn, symbol of goodness and strength, and bending put the corn to his lips. Then he placed his lips to the baby's forehead, and laid the corn at the infant's side. Juan Celo acted as godfather in the place of his son, who was absent on a railroad job.

The godmother received the congratulations of friends, their left hands on one another's shoulders, and exchanged good wishes. . . .

—BILLY HESCH, in *The New Mexico Sentinel*, June 1, 1939

T HE PUEBLO or town-dwelling Indians are a gentle
and cautious people, by nature more Christian
than we are. Christian teachings contain ideas they
find sympathetic, and Catholicism and their own
nature-religion can live side by side, even if they do
not mingle. At the heart of each faith is the feeling
that man is helpless by himself, but can find help by
his ways of living and worshiping, if his ways are what
they should be. For the Pueblo, religion is bound to
be largely anticipatory and placative, but in essence,
like all Indian religion, it is pure worship.

The United States fought a duel to the death with
Apaches that cost us in only ten years of it (1861-
1870) $40,000,000 and 1,000 lives; but the Pueblos
have never suffered violence from us, nor offered us
violence. You hear various explanations for their survival. But everyone agrees that they have made a good
job of themselves during the ages, despite their periods
of exile and their massacres at the hands of Apache,
Navajo, Comanche, Ute, and Spaniard. They have
nurtured the ability to keep on adapting and keep on
hoping. It makes them an impressive people, and the
Southwest thinks about them a good deal.

The Pueblos were here in the first place, had arrived, and were installed. Long before the Apaches
came they were living in well-built villages along the

Rio Grande and out on the westward mesas. When Oñate came up the Rio Grande to San Juan, certain Apaches were living at a near-by place called Navajo. They were never like other Apaches again; they began to learn things of the Pueblos, they opened up an instinct in themselves of being willing to learn, and of knowing the kind of thing they were after. It was about 1200 that the Apaches began to split into two families, the bright cousins and the dumb cousins. The dumb cousins were those who developed military genius, and the others (who found something else to develop) began to be called the Navajo.

There was a time when even the Pueblos were tenderfeet in the Southwest. Before them a race of Indians had arrived, set up a way of life, and disappeared. Today we are studying the traces of those Indians and wondering why they disappeared. When a race disappears everyone wants to know why. In the Southwest it seems to be everyone's business because people have a lurking fear about their own future. The tree rings disclose that a drought came in 1276 and lasted till 1300; if such a drought came again and stayed a quarter of a century, who would be left in the entire region? The railroads could bring water in, of course, but the inhabitants would soon have enough of life under such conditions and move away, the ranchers first of all.

Those Indians who disappeared, the Mimbreños,

may have taught the Pueblos a good deal. The Pueblos made good use of all the help they could get. People who know about such matters say the Pueblos were builders as well as dancers, and that in Arkansas you can see stone ruins they left on their successive slow stages of exile to the Rio Grande. They raised corn and harvested the crop for the winter. It made them different from the hunting Indians of the Plains. The hunting Indians began to hunt the Pueblos when the winters were long and hard, according to the law of human nature that you go and get food when you are desperate. The Pueblos, understanding this law, made the corn storeroom the center of their houses and built rooms above and round it, so that all the houses in a village became forts to protect the corn. Then they built a wall to make the whole village a fortress, too. They used ladders to reach the roofs of their houses, which they entered through a hole in the roof, and they pulled the outside ladders up with them. The more tricks the hunting Indians thought of to get the corn, the more tricks the Pueblos countered with. The Pueblos knew what a corn storeroom meant—a winter without anxiety, a winter when you can stay at home and feel safe, and think about making pottery and blankets, and tell stories, and sing songs, and make love, and play with the babies, and meditate on life, and improve your prayer-dances. If you can work hard all summer and rest hard all winter, life begins to mean things. But life is not good if you are never sure of your food, the way the hunting Indians live; even the weather is your enemy then.

Nobody knows how early the Pueblo Indian devoted himself to the corn, but it was his greatest achievement, and it may be that no people anywhere has achieved anything greater. The corn gave him the kind of life he wanted, and he began to find subtle and lovely meanings in that corn-given life.

An Isleta Indian told Elsie Clews Parsons about one of their times of ceremonial prayer, coming down from long-ago centuries. "We have four days inside getting ready," he said. "On the fourth night we perform the ceremony; then we have four outside days, during which we may not touch a woman or kill anything, not even an insect, or hurt anybody's feelings."

This Isleta Indian told Mrs. Parsons also about a young man who was made a cacique but was too full of energy and too restless for a sacrificial life, and so went out into the landscape to chop wood. The young man heard an invisible voice telling him the end had come for him because of his disobedience.

"I told you at the beginning not to work, not to kill anything, not to hurt anybody's heart or feelings."

If he has a good stock of corn, and a well-built house, and time for prayer and play, a man can afford to think about the heart and the feelings of other people and make such distinctions.

People who live near the Pueblos will tell you that nobody can fathom the Indian's mind, and then by an inexplicable feat they proceed to fathom the Indian's mind for you. The only people I ever hear talk about Indians who make them convincingly human are those who have lived with them in their houses and towns. In 1924 a young woman named Jane Henderson came down from Denver to one of the Pueblos to learn the Pueblo way of singing. Studying music in Paris, she had become interested in primitive themes, and when she came back she decided to go to a Pueblo to study Indian singing. A warm personality, with a love of people and their ways, she picked herself up out of Denver, home, and friendships, and with pleasure and interest settled down in an archaic Indian village where she did not know a syllable of the language.

We have a complicated system of musical notation; the Pueblos have no system at all, and simply pass their songs along from person to person, or from generation to generation. So our attempt to obtain and use their themes is rather hopeless. Our instruments are not adequate tools; if you wish to add the Indian drum to a string quartette you resort to the 'cello, but the 'cello is far from an Indian drum. It has no heartbeat. Nor can you make sure of Indian pauses through our system of musical notation. So, after she had lived at the Pueblo for a time, Jane Henderson decided to learn the Indian songs as they were sung, for their

beauty in themselves, and without thought of record-
ing them. She learned many songs. She still knows
them; their evanescent and precious beauty is a delight to hear. (She is Mrs. Gustave Baumann now, and
lives in Santa Fe.)

If you are responsive to laughter and tears, music,
color, movement, and form, you can enter into the
daily life of the Pueblos without a jar to them or
to yourself. In degree we can visualize Pueblo
life through archaeologists and pottery experts; but
through the singer, I think, comes a picture more com-
prehensible.

It was not a happy household Jane came to live
with, for the mother had died not long before. The
family consisted of four children, the grandmother
Serafina, and an uncle Rafael. But Jane sang at her
work, and the others began little by little to sing, too.
Then friends of Rafael's would drop in in the evening
and sing and help her learn what they were singing.
They lived on the plaza of the village; all pueblos
have a plaza, for it is there the dances are held. Sometimes the houses are not on the plaza; perhaps there
are too many houses for that.

Jane said she often helped Rafael saw wood. She
said there was little difference really in the sawing of
wood, the rocking of a baby to sleep, and the polishing of pottery; all have the same rhythm and are fundamental, and not long to do at a time. At night Sera-

fina put the little children to bed on the floor of the kitchen. Her silhouette on the wall over the stove loomed up large or became small as she moved before the lamp, but it always had the same simple qualities of form as herself. Jane slept in the adjoining room, Rafael on a cot at the foot of her iron bed, and in the morning there was the unforgettable sound of Serafina's white doeskin moccasins, as she tiptoed in and touched him on the shoulder.

The baby cried every pause in the night's breeze, and the sick little sister coughed most of the night. Soft voices replied to each other from one room to another: sounds like these—*Ge-ha-o-chi-ki-la-ga?*

The sick child sat by the stove, a green and yellow checked dress against the pink adobe wall, and Serafina in the next room or out-of-doors would keep murmuring to her. Sometimes at night Jane slipped out of bed and into the kitchen, tiptoeing over the sleepers, and took the child in her arms or gave her a drink of water. She grew no better, and one evening she died. Serafina did not hum at her work for a long time after that. Jane watched the uncle receive condolences from his neighbors or his American friends from Santa Fe, one hand held out to them, while he covered his eyes with the other, and bowed his head. The day of the funeral, far off on the edge of the village coming up over a little hill a man was carrying something white, much as one would tenderly present a gift. He was followed by a chorus singing a dirge. There had been few men in the plaza all day; they had been singing somewhere for the child.

Pueblo men often act as nursemaids. It was a common sight on a cold winter morning to see them standing smoking cigarettes in the plaza in the early sun, with a blanketed baby on their backs, the other children clustering about them. Men and children were together a great deal.

Beginning nine nights before Christmas, every night in front of each house would be a small square of ocote (pitch-pine) faggots, piled one on top of another about two feet tall. At the t-a-n-g t-a-n-g of the church bell, which an Indian rang standing on the flat church roof, the fire was quickly lighted from a few sticks burning in readiness. The period of awaiting the solemn t-a-n-g t-a-n-g was exciting. Everybody jumped to pop the burning sticks into the pile of faggots, which then shot up in the blinding though smoky blaze that ocote gives, filling the plaza with shadow and silhouette.

The blasé and discontented might well have seen Serafina's kitchen in the evening. Who said there was nothing of interest in this world with its crust of ashes and center of fire? The family made itself comfortable round the stove, the cradle swinging from large wooden beams near enough for one of the group to give it a swing when the baby waked and cried. The baby had her grandmother's scarf over her. Jane sat

near Tonita polishing pottery, and Rafael in a chair
threaded needles for the younger children to string
beads with. Often the group worked with clay, each
after his own fashion, and Jane said the tie was a
miracle that bound them all together, with the clay
bowls and water before them, and pieces of gourd
floating in the water to form the shapes with. Past
seven o'clock they talked and laughed; the jokes were
repeated over and over, till the last bit of laughter was
extracted from them. They watched their great sculp-
tress, Serafina, spin and turn bowl after bowl on her
nimble hands. But the tie was severed when the pottery was finished and placed under the stove to dry.
Everyone washed his hands, and as the water was
thrown away (out the door) so was the bond that
held the group together. A few moments later, as she
came in to take the brilliant blankets off Rafael's cot
to place them on the kitchen floor, Serafina walked
through the room a stranger again, the shadow of an
alien race and tongue. To Jane her soft padded feet
seemed to say, "I know you no more."

Dinner was a great time for song at the pueblo. At
Serafina's they sang the basket songs at supper, in the
slant of a slow-setting sun which colored the whole
sky. The dances were like a wall of beauty Jane could
never go behind nor understand. They were a horizontal band of images across the breadth of her con-

sciousness, frieze after frieze of figures colored and costumed and masked, sounding little bells as they paced or leapt, gesturing with piñon sprays—like sand paintings come to life, or a picture-writing done in the plaza with living bodies. They brought to the village a harmony she did not know how to share.

As the time approached for her return to Denver, an old man with a sense of humor composed a song for her: "She has gone far away to her pueblo called Demba—that's where Snowflower lives—and when we think of her it's with a heartfelt feeling, and when she gets up in the morning and scratches herself—and scratches herself—I guess she will think of us."

Young Pueblos must find it disturbing to reconcile their traditional and their contemporary life. But they do not wear their hearts on their sleeves. They go to the government Indian school for seven months of the year, and at school last winter they were producing a Gilbert and Sullivan operetta. Not long ago when the best high-school bands of northern New Mexico paraded for honors in the streets of Santa Fe, the band from the Indian school performed as well as any of them. The boys play football and have track meets, and are as casual and communicative as any other boys their age. There is every reason why they should become "Americans." But you think about the future when you see these same young people in summer dancing the sacred dances in the plaza of their villages. And you feel a good deal of sympathy, for the problem of past, present and future is not the Indian's only.

8. Maize

Corn has no serious competitor on alkalied, subbed [sub-irrigated], light, or unleveled lands. Under irrigation it will grow on land too rough for cereals, and in dry-farm areas, on soils too sandy or arid for crops other than sorghums and beans. It may be successfully produced with fifteen inches or less rainfall. . . .

—*Corn Culture,* by GEORGE R. QUESENBERRY,
Bulletin, New Mexico College of Agriculture

To WRITE about the Southwest is to write about the Pueblo Indians, and to write about them is to write about maize, for maize has made them what they are. Their mythologies warn them never to stop "watching, beseeching, and caring for the corn-flesh." The Pueblo of Santa Clara is swept before corn is fetched home from harvest, "because corn is just the same as people and must have the plaza clean." None of the Pueblos plant corn as they plant other crops; it must be planted by all the men together, and harvested in the same communal fashion. At Zuñi there is a saying, "Love and cherish your corn as you love and cherish your women." To the Pueblo, corn has al-

ways been the seed of seeds, and nothing compares
with it in mystery and importance, or in a curious
human-ness.

The Pueblo Indians do not make so sharp a distinction as we do between the animate and inanimate
worlds. Into their dealings with the non-human they
carry over their ways in human relations. The spirit
and behavior which cause good results in dealing with
people they make use of in dealing with the other
living or non-living objects of the world, and with the
world itself as a collection of forces. Reverence, gentle-
ness, patience, assiduity are Pueblo characteristics.
They resort to magic at times to counteract and control the fear of sorcery which is with them always,
though no reason for it has ever been uncovered.
Magic practices, though, are not a vital part of their
culture. Magic may bring good luck, and therefore
it should not be neglected. The Pueblos resemble us
with our astrologers and numerologists, and our superstitions about signs.

In the feeling of the Indian toward his corn there
is no desire to enforce his will upon the external world.
His belief that all objects possess a natural vitality becomes philosophic and religious in the ascription of
life to nature as a whole. This feeling attains great
beauty in the corn ceremonies at Zuñi, which pantomime the rise of corn from among the lowly grasses of
the earth. The Rain Youth and each Dew Maiden in

turn clasp between them the tasseled wild grass and lift it higher and higher, till their linked effort and the prayer of their mingling transform it into corn. Upon the corn-plant therefore the embrace of man leaves something of the semblance of his body; even his fingerprints can be seen at the joints of the stalk. More striking still, as the ceremonial chant continues, where man and girl touch the plants at their middles, new ears of kernels, of human origin, spring out in witness of their parentage and draped, in the corn silk, with the very hair of human marriageableness.

This ceremony not only has human significance, it is botanically correct; for the startling peculiarity of corn is that it is created by man instead of by nature. Other cereals can get along somehow without cultivation; uncultivated corn sinks back into an insignificant wild grass. And the Inca, the Aztec, the Pueblo, the American Indian in general with his circumspection about corn and unflagging interest in it, has discovered a good many things about it. Not only must corn be hoed continually, it must be planted in double rows. It is an outgoing, marrying, co-operative plant, and no individualist. It will not tolerate self-fertilization. The ears may have eight or twelve or more rows of kernels, but only an even number. Unlike other plants it has two sets of seeds, the ears and the seed-tassels; it has also two kinds of flowers, the male bearing the stamens and forming the tassels, the female bearing the pistils and constituting the silk. And there is a silk for every kernel.

Corn has also a most elastic nature, and this is another of man's great good fortunes. Frost is fatal to any and all of its five hundred named species, but the plant compensates by growing at high as well as at low altitudes, and in dry as well as moist climates. Farm books will tell you that this tropical plant requires rich black soil and will use any amount of manuring. Yet in New Mexico, a state not designed by Providence for agriculture, corn is the most important crop. The Pueblo Indian has developed in his long cultivation a variety of dwarf corn with long roots that is sure to mature and to yield a harvest even in dry years, if they are not too frightfully dry. His diligence is slow and intensive, and he does not cultivate wide areas. Like all other corn-growing tribes, through the breeding and care of open-pollinated plants he has fashioned the variety that suits his need and taste.

Among our states (1929), only Iowa and Illinois produce more corn than does Argentina; Rumania surpasses Nebraska, and Russia surpasses Ohio, Minnesota, or Kansas. Mexico, Hungary, India, and Egypt produce about the same amount apiece as Texas. And the figures of corn-production in states of the corn-belt are staggering: they are whole continents of self-sufficiency in themselves, we are a nation that need

never lack for food. Our poverty is fantastic, in view
of the corn-belt. It is the most important single source
of human food in the United States, though indirectly,
because nearly all the crop goes to hogs, poultry, and
cattle in the form of bran, ensilage, fodder, gluten
feed and meal, and oil cake. Four-fifths of our corn is
a stock food on the farm that produces it; nothing indi-
cates better what a stabilizing influence, what a quiet
unthought-of form of wealth it is. In the world-diet
rice feeds more people; but since our botanists and
chemists, following the example of the Indian, began
to "watch, beseech, and care for the corn-flesh," corn
is yielding a number of allied products which with
rice would be unthinkable.

My uncle Dan, when he comes back every year or
so from the Philippines, asks for his favorite dessert,
Indian pudding. With such a multitude of corn dishes
we may each have our favorites. My own are blue-
cornmeal muffins, spoonbread, corn soufflé, and corn
chowder. They seem to me among the most agreeable
dishes in the world, and I am glad that everybody can
afford them, for they are not in the least plebeian. People who look down on corn dishes don't know how to
prepare them. I never knew a European who had the
slightest feeling for corn. But I have read that the
English King and Queen, when they came to America,
took to cornbread with apparent liking. As a boy I
liked cornmeal pancakes made with sour milk better

than any dish I have known since. In the Southwest Mrs. C. M. Fergusson of Albuquerque has acquainted me with a delicious gruel called atole, made of blue-cornmeal and warm milk. Other native and Indian corn dishes appeal to me somewhat less, tostadas for example, or tortillas, tamales, pesole. Cornbread and cornmeal gems and corn syrup I imagine everybody likes. Counting up the number of corn dishes every-body knows, I can think of these additional ones: hoe cake, Johnny cake, hot mush, fried mush, corn pone, corn fritters, succotash, parched corn, cornstarch pud-ding, and the various Battle Creek blends. There are also corn-cob pipes and Bourbon whiskey. In parts of New Mexico a farm is known as a sixty- or eighty-gallon farm, according to the amount of corn whiskey it is good for.

The Inca and Aztec civilizations, although produc-ing ingots of gold and silver, were rendered stable only by their maize. Certain of the conquistadores who survived the terrific expeditions did well for them-selves, and their exertions did well indeed for his Catholic Majesty; but Spain's dream of untold wealth across the ocean came true unexpectedly, in this cereal named Zea mays.

The chief benefit of the corn has always been psy-chological, however, in its effect on those who work with it, the feeling of wonder and gratitude archaic

man has known at each step of its response to his efforts. It would be a story for De Kruif to tell, if it were
possible to know it from the beginning, full of drama
and of instruction.

But we shall probably never know it from the beginning. There is a species of wild grass called teosinte
(teocentli), which flourishes on the uplands of middle
America. This teosinte has two varieties, and they
are the only wild relatives of the maize closely enough
related to interbreed freely with it. They cannot be
used as food, the grains are few, are hidden in horny
chaff, and must be pried out of a woody rachis. If the
Guatemalans or Mexicans bred the maize from this
unfriendly plant, they surpassed all primitive peoples
in their skill as gardeners, as well as all modern botanists. For today experiments with teosinte get one nowhere. And to assume that maize was derived from
teosinte, one must assume too that teosinte was a cul-
tivated plant. It is hard to believe that it is or ever was
of use to man except for forage, and the early Mexicans had no animals which required forage. On the
other hand, it is hard to believe that maize came into
existence independently of teosinte. It would have
taken a long time—twenty thousand years would
hardly do.

Dated monuments bear witness to man's life in
America back to about the time of Christ. Ears of corn
left by the Basketmakers of the Southwest, and those

in prehistoric caves of South America, prove that maize was completely domesticated and the worship of the corn under full swing at a much earlier date. Maize has had a remarkable longevity, in any case. The Indian corn found by the first explorers was practically what we have now. Remains of ears in prehistoric caves duplicate our present varieties. There is a vague chance that some Aztec legend or Mayan scupture may throw light on the mystery. Or, as the serious study of food and drug plants of the Americas progresses, something may come to light. Up to the present not a quarter of our drug plants and fewer than half of our food plants have been examined by scientifically trained culturists; and there is sobering risk that the rapid abandonment of their primitive culture by the Indians may lose us important knowledge.

Meanwhile, corn keeps on being wonderful in its response to man, and the people who work with it keep on being wonderful, too. For many years George Harrison Shull, a man of genius and Professor of Botany and Genetics at Princeton University, has been engaged on artificial pollination. In 1905 he developed a practical method based on Mendel's law. Now, by covering tassels and silk with paper bags to prevent natural fertilization, and then pollinating the stalks by hand, growers can inbreed uniform strains, and these in turn they can cross to produce a hybrid that will yield from ten to thirty per cent more an acre than the open-pollinated varieties. The competition among seed companies is so brisk as a result that one such concern dispatches experimental seed to South America by plane to eliminate winter and to speed up results. In 1937 hybrid corn amounted to a mere four per cent of the crop. But in 1940 it represented 42 per cent. And the winner of the De Kalb, Illinois, hybrid corn-growing contest in 1940, William Mentjes of Le Center, Minnesota, got 157.69 bushels to the acre —five and a half times the national average.

Dr. Shull has never received a cent in royalties for his discoveries. His one wish is that his experiments may secure money enough "to establish a separate department of botany" at Princeton.

9. Oñate

Our men . . . threw themselves into the water and drank as though the entire river could not quench their terrible thirst. Satisfied, they threw themselves down like drunken wretches on a tavern floor, swollen and more like toads than men.

—GASPAR PÉREZ DE VILLAGRÁ, *Historia de Nueva Mexico*

VILLAGRÁ, a devoted officer of Juan de Oñate, so describes in his historical poem the arrival of Oñate's expedition at the Rio Grande, probably at a spot fifteen miles below El Paso.

The expedition knew extreme thirst again while crossing the Jornado del Muerto. This eighty-mile stretch with no sign of water the Spaniards called the journey of death because it often proved itself to be so. Tradition says that near by Pueblo Indians saved the lives of Oñate's people, giving them water and corn at the northern end of the hot waste of gravel and red adobe earth, and that the Spaniards called the place Socorro (succor) on that account.

Oñate's expedition fifty-eight years after Coronado began the real colonizing of the Southwest, but it was consistently luckless, and the source of its misfortune was the character of Oñate himself. Once I was driving with Gustave Baumann in the Painted Desert country. It was a place where everything was parallel and long shadows from the clouds streaked the mesa and buttes. Baumann said, "I met an old prospector here a long time ago. He had three burros. He was riding one, his duds were on the others. He had a small dog in a tin bucket. Was going right across country. Nowhere in particular—those fellows work on hunches. I took some photos of him. I wanted to sketch him, but he said he was in a hurry to get wherever it was he was going."

It may have been the state of mind of Juan de Oñate. Everything he did he did in a hurry. Colonizing, though his ostensible purpose, was a side issue with him. He had the prospector's faith that somewhere and somehow the earth would give him a handout. Or rather, another handout; it had already given him one. He was a miner, and the mines at Zacatecas had made him a millionaire. This northward expedition to quiet his prospector's itch cost him a million pesos. After Coronado, the viceroys no longer supplied subsidies, and anyone going north had to pay his way. To a good many documentary accounts of failure of one kind or another, in the archives, is appended the ironic statement, "This I accomplished at my own expense."

Like Coronado, Oñate brought stock along. But he brought a great many more, and particularly females for breeding. He started out with 7,000 head (cattle, sheep, goats, and horses) and 83 teams of oxen. He also had 400 colonists (the children riding on top of the oxcarts), seven friars, and 120 soldiers.

Everyone was eager to settle down as soon as possible, and the river at Albuquerque appeared promising, with flat lands (though marshy) and tall cottonwoods. But Oñate continued on up the stream to the garden spot of the northern valley, where the Chama flows into the Rio Grande. The pueblo of Kay-Pa was situated there, and he persuaded the Indians to give him their village and build a new one. They agreed, not being in a position to disagree, and he rewarded them handsomely by naming their new village San Juan de los Caballeros (St. John of the Gentlemen). His own village he named San Gabriel.

This region, which they reached July 11, 1598, has been almost continuously inhabited by colonists ever since.

Oñate's first act was to make sure of water. Like all newcomers he thought it was possible to make sure of it. Within three days he had his men and a thousand Indians digging irrigation ditches. After water, his thoughts turned to God. Within two weeks he had a fine new chapel ready, and at its dedication he put on a fiesta in the form of a sham battle between the

Moors and the Christians. (This fiesta is still given annually at Mora.) The Indians responded more favorably to this entertainment than to anything else the visitors had done. Tradition says Oñate thought of this battle as a way to head off mutiny among his men, who were getting tired of his fever-pitch. The day after the battle the general called together the governors of the pueblos and with a grand gesture apportioned their sixty villages to his seven friars to be christianized.

A month later he decided he had done enough for the colonists and reverted to his prospecting, the real reason for the expedition. Now he was entitled to his fun, if prospecting be fun. Many a ghost town in the Southwest even today has two or three inhabitants, men still searching for a lode that disappeared in the boom-time years ago. Oñate ordered Captain Zaldivar to start out eastward with sixty men. He himself took a jaunt of several hundred miles circling Pecos and the Manzano mountains. He had no sooner returned to San Gabriel than he started out again, going westward to Acoma and even to the Hopi villages. He sent one captain further still, to look for some mines he had heard about. His energy is remarkable, though at this distance it is hard to say whether it was due to thyroid or to altitude. The colonists were without the stimulant, whatever it was, that kept him at it, and they grew more and more dissatisfied. Nonetheless,

Oñate sent requests back to Mexico City for more and more soldiers and more and more friars, and then struck out across the Great Plains for the fabled Quivira Coronado had investigated. His investigation likewise proved in vain. This time when he returned the irrigation ditches were empty. So was the chapel. San Gabriel was almost deserted, both colonists and priests having fled from a great drought. If leaders don't think of them, people must think for themselves. Even the Indians were subsisting on seeds.

Ross Calvin of Silver City, reflecting on this curious story, and on the fact that Oñate or his successor founded Santa Fe in 1608, and that this town "uniquely old among American cities" still remains "uniquely small among them," is led to wonder what would have happened if Oñate had marched up the Gila instead of up the Rio Grande, and founded Silver City instead of Santa Fe. At Silver City there is a valley which in the 1870's yielded white silver from one lode as fast as it could be taken out, to the extent of $5,000,000. "What would it not have done for the perpetually bankrupt little colony at Santa Fe!" exclaims Calvin in his excellent book, *Sky Determines*. "The total wealth of the colony through its whole history could not hold a candle to it. Instead of poverty, isolation, peonage, there would have been wealth, progress, growth, and the flowering of a native culture."

The truth is that when the caballeros and the colonists entered the Southwest driving along their stock,
they brought with them the source of most of the little wealth their descendants have ever known. For
generations sheep and steers were to be the only export of a people who needed to import tools, clothing,
equipment, a thousand things that make life easy, and
who could never afford to do so.

When it grew apparent in Mexico City that the
north country would never make returns on the heavy
investment of the expeditions, the authorities did not
on that account give it up. They took their religion too
seriously to do so. This northern outpost seemed to
them worth maintaining as a base for converting the
Indians. But the conversion of the Indians did not
really prosper, either, and the padres who came to
convert the Indians remained to solace the colonists
in the long separation from the mother-culture.

The Spaniards came to find wealth. They found
none; in their cattle, sheep, and goats they merely
brought their grub along. Well for their descendants,
it was a source of food that kept multiplying. To the
larder of the Indians it was a most welcome addition,
also. Further, as everyone knows, the horses and sheep
which got away from Coronado and Oñate were the
first of their kind in the north country. They began
a revolution in the customs and folkways of a dozen
tribes of Indians, and at the same time established the

pastoral nature of subsequent Spanish life in New Mexico. Ultimately the horse made possible the deadly perfection of Apache warfare. The horse and sheep made of the Navajo a nation that rivaled the Spaniard in the Southwest, and that might even have expelled him from the country if the United States had not moved in. The way the Navajo welcomed horses and sheep and changed at once into a nation of horsemen and shepherds makes it seem possible that the Spaniards obligingly restored to them what their forefathers had been forced to leave behind on the uplands of Mongolia centuries before, when they came across Bering Sea on the ice.

Recently the total civic budget of the thirteen cities of New Mexico (as apart from towns and villages) was $1,368,000. The figure gives an idea of the lack of wealth in the State. An eastern city founded a long time after Santa Fe, called New York, had a budget for the same period of $581,000,000. The total of all possible property on which New Mexico might assess taxes fell far below such a figure. But in the 1940 census New Mexico was, for whatever reason, the fastest-growing state except for Florida. In ten years New Mexico had increased 24.9 per cent, and Arizona 14.3. These two states now have 528,000 and 497,000 people respectively.

10. Two Centuries and More

On the afternoon of August 18, 1846, Gen. Kearney, in command of the United States army, marched into the town and ended the rule of the Mexican government in New Mexico. On the morning of August 19th, he made the following address to the people gathered in the Plaza:

"NEW MEXICANS: We have come with peaceable intentions and kind feelings toward you all . . . to better your condition and make you a part of the Republic of the United States. We mean not to murder you or rob you of your property.

". . . In our country . . . the Catholic and the Protestant are esteemed alike. Every man has a right to serve God according to his heart. . . . We esteem the most peaceable man, the best man.

"I advise you to attend to your domestic pursuits, cultivate industry, be peaceable and obedient to the laws. Do not resort to violent means to correct abuses. . . . Armijo is no longer your governor. His power has departed; but he will return and be as one of you. When he shall return you are not to molest him.

"It is my intention to continue in office those by whom you have been governed, except the governor. I am your governor. Henceforth look to me for protection."

Response was made by Juan Bautista Vigil y Alarid, the official left in charge by Governor Armijo, who had departed for Chihuahua on August 16th, leaving the town open for General Kearney to take possession without bloodshed.

"GENERAL: . . . It is for us to obey and respect the established authorities, no matter what may be our private opinions.

"The inhabitants of this department humbly present their allegiance to the government of North America. No one in this world can successfully resist the power of him who is stronger. Do not find it strange if there has been no joy or enthusiasm in seeing our city occupied by your military forces. To us the power of the Mexican Republic is dead. No matter what our condition, she was our mother. What child will not shed abundant tears at the tomb of his parents? Civil war is the cursed source of that deadly poison which has spread over one of the grandest and greatest countries ever created. Today we belong to a great and powerful nation. We are cognizant of your kindness, of your courtesy, and that of your troops; we know that we belong to the republic that owes its origin to the immortal Washington, whom all civilized nations admire and respect. How different would be our situation had we been invaded by European nations! We are aware of the unfortunate condition of the Poles. . . ."

—Santa Fe New Mexican

KEARNY'S remarks are characteristic of their time and of the way most U. S. Americans talked up to 1929. Since 1929 our point of view has changed enough to make such a speech seem halfway back to the French Revolution, with its emphasis on religious freedom and equality of opportunity. As though all you had to do about democracy was to set it up and start it going and it would go forever. And we could all be free to go off and do as we pleased. For democracy then seemed to us self-operative, independent of us and we of it. We did not need to practice it every minute. We did not need to pitch in and help, all of us. To bring democracy to the Mexican Southwest, we thought, was indeed to bring it a wonderful gift.

And it is clear from the words of Vigil y Alarid that he is inclined to take somewhat the same view of it. His reference to Washington implies as much. The contrast he makes between conquered New Mexico and conquered Poland is even more true today. His reference to Old Mexico is full of genuine feeling, and should be noted. But on the whole he seems to grant that democracy may be a better form of government than what the Southwest had been getting. Under Armijo Mexican rule had certainly reached a new low point of dreadfulness.

And now, a century later—has democracy been a success in the Southwest? And what of the future?

There is a story of Padre Martinez of Taos, who was an advanced man in many ways and who printed the first book in the Southwest, a speller. When the young men asked him what kind of government the United States was, he said it was a republic, and added that a republic was "a burro on which lawyers jog along better than priests." Perhaps he had to explain to them what a lawyer was, for in 1831 there was not a lawyer in New Mexico (and only one physician). It was a fair enough warning that with the U. S. soldiers was coming also a life which had far more exactitude to it than the Southwest had dreamt of. The common people here had never caught sight of money, hardly knew what it was, and had no need of it, before the wagon trains came. The borders of ranches were vague. The science of bookkeeping was unknown.

One must get a bird's-eye view, too, of the history of the region since Oñate. On the heels of that effervescent figure came a resolute and efficient colonization from Mexico City. Then came an equally resolute rebellion by the Indians who, tired of having Christianity thrust down their throats, drove out every living Spaniard. Then came an efficient reconquest, and several centuries of solidification, and the establishment of a way of life by the Spanish colonials in the huge room of the Southwest, hermetically sealed so far as any vital touch went with the life they had left behind in Mexico and Spain.

My wife speaks of all Spanish soldiers and conquerors of New Mexico as De Vargas. And Don Diego de Vargas, the hero of the reconquest, is typical of them all, and it makes at least for simplification to telescope them. The successive governors of the province seem also to have been wave after wave of the same thing, though one mysterious and charming figure steps in in the person of Peñalosa, to let you feel the goodness of finding a real human being in the maze of bureaucracy an empire breeds even in its outposts. This Peñalosa had been born in South America; he was a rare official, not sent over from Spain, but native-born and full of native awarenesses. In the course of treating the Indians as people he encountered the hostility of the Inquisition. Summoned back to Mexico City, he was not burned at the stake, but he did have to walk the streets in public humiliation. Full of resentment that creaturely kindness should disgrace him and strip him of wealth and lands, Peñalosa shook the dust of New Spain from his shoes, and went to France. There with the co-operation of the French court, he was able to think up a number of ways of keeping the Emperor of Spain awake at night. We know little about him, for the records were destroyed in the rebellion. But when one comes to his name in the portentous list of governors on the walls of the Old Palace, one can· think, *that* governor anyway was probably a good fellow, an American, one of us.

Through the days of the Spanish governors, the rich colonists were growing richer, the poor colonists poorer, the priests lazier and more avaricious. The Navajo preyed on the rich, who in turn preyed on the poor, and the poor could prey on nobody. Every now and then the rich men would organize a revenge party and kill a number of Navajo, and bring back slaves if the boys were strong and the girls good-looking. The Navajo took captives also, and altogether there was an amount of racial intermingling.

The landowners, the ricos (the rich ones), developed a life of their own. They were like a group shipwrecked on an island, or dropped from another planet on an inaccessible portion of the earth. Probably the ricos in California led a somewhat similar existence, though it would be far less dangerous, and they had an ocean at hand and boats went to and from Mexico. Otherwise our history offers nothing like this southwestern life that centered along the road from Socorro to Bernalillo, in the wide river valley that has the Sandia and Manzano mountains to the south.

The great low houses stood on either side of the road, shaded by cottonwoods, and fortified against marauding Navajo. They contained little furniture, because the ricos had no way of importing pieces consonant with their wealth and dignity. There were no cabinet-makers in the colony, and there was always a staggering lack of tools for any and every purpose. The tables and chairs were of native workmanship. The floor was of earth well beaten down, and generally people preferred to sit on it, on Navajo rugs. You had an idea of a man's wealth from his rugs. There were few bedsteads, and mattresses stood against the adobe walls during the day, covered with rugs or shawls.

The ricos were sociable, and families saw much of one another. The favorite hour was in the late afternoon, the time for chocolate. The men wore buckskin dyed black, with silver buttons; their clothes were well tailored. They had long hair and wore queues; full beards and mustaches were the fashion. They acquired a habit from the Indians of wearing a blanket over the shoulder, a brightly colored and costly serape such as one still sees in Old Mexico. New Mexico Indians still come to town with a blanket, and it is a perfect way of dressing for a climate like that of the Southwest. The women had low-cut bodices and short woolen skirts of lively color, and they always carried a shawl. This reboso showed a woman's caste as the serape showed the man's. The shawl is another perfect garment, and many American women in this climate wish they could wear them. In 1875 Martha Summerhayes, in the Arizona heat with her officer husband during the Apache wars, would have flung aside her entire New York and Paris outfit for native dress, but the lieutenant forbade it. Her account of her experiences, *Vanished Arizona,* should be reprinted; it has a thousand excellences. Mabel Dodge Luhan of Taos (she spells her name differently from her husband in order to aid Eastern readers to pronounce Lujan) longs for the "insulation" of the shawl, and wears hers whenever she can; she has come to dread the "exposed, revealed, open" way U. S. American women dress.

The world of the ricos was a man's world and so was not especially good for men and not at all good for women. The father had absolute power over his family and peons and slaves. The sons, like their father, enjoyed considerable immunity from misdeeds, because a law of the colony said that priests and officers in the army could only be tried by their peers. There were probably only a thousand of the ricos in all, perhaps a fiftieth of the population, but they were autocrats and tyrants in every sense of the word. Men had a smattering of education, but in the whole Southwest there was not a single school for girls. Girls were married early, and began to bear children. There were five meals a day, three of them heavy ones; and few women rode horseback. They did no housework, and it would seem as though their only exercise was dancing. The diet and the indolent life did not make for lissomeness, and often too by thirty, childbearing would leave a woman ailing. Riding along the Socorro road I have often wondered about those girls and women. When the great electrical storms come in summer, and the lightning palpitates through the trees and above the mountains, were their hearts circumscribed by the routine of their lives, or did living tendrils elude the parochial and the semi-Moorish, and reach out with hope for the clear direction and intelligent joy that come when the differences between the sexes are minimized instead of exaggerated?

The young men went away two or three times a year. They went to the plains to kill buffalo and bring back the dried meat for the year's supply. They went to Chihuahua to trade and to sell their sheep, a distance of six hundred miles. Perhaps they went to Taos as the yearly Taos fair grew in importance as a place of barter and news. They were superb horsemen, brave and tireless fighters. They had manners, and manner.

The life of the ricos was full of incident, passion, romance, and death. It had its own grace, evanescent as lightning. It was lived minute by minute, and left behind it no memoirs and few letters by which we might summon it up before our eyes. It was unrelated and irresponsible, and every one of the great houses that faced the highway during the seventeenth and eighteenth centuries has vanished. It is unique in being the one form of living in the Southwest that has left no ruins. All you can do is to form a vague picture of what it might have felt like to be out of touch with the world, to have no knowledge of the books and music and art that stirred the mother-country during those generations—and yet to have enough gaiety, love, hate, and danger all about to intoxicate you with a life lived to consume itself.

Harvey Fergusson, in his *Rio Grande,* has a chapter on the ricos which reads like a poem; he says he learned what he knows from the old men and women he listened to in his boyhood in Albuquerque. There was no other source for him to go to. Nina Otero Warren has written a small book about the life of the ricos, which also reads like a poem. She too listened to the talk of old men and women, and she possesses fragmentary records of her forefathers and their relatives.

Wealth and privilege are circumstances to which people must adapt themselves as soberly as they do to hardship and famine, if they are to survive. The ricos might have made it and not gone under, if as a class the men had united their consciousness with that of their women. Under the stress of that life the women developed rare qualities of compassion and self-sacrifice; half slaves themselves they could feel the sufferings of the common people. The paisanos, the small landowners, had to depend on their rich and powerful compadres, the ricos, for their very lives. The Navajo would rarely attack a hacienda, but they harried the poor year after year, and thus the paisanos came to live under the shadow of the great houses. To survive drought and Indians, they fell into debt to the ricos. They became peons, the ricos their patróns. They never could get out of debt. And even so the ricos as a whole did little to help them against the Indians, or against pestilence and drought.

The peons no doubt nourished a secret hatred of their masters, and were ready to welcome the U. S. Americans as they came west, first as trappers, then with wagon trains to trade, and finally as soldiers to possess the country. The only paisanos who escaped being peons were those in the mountain villages and in the less accessible portions of the upper Rio Grande

Valley. They were too poor for the Navajo to bother
with; it was too much trouble to go where they lived.

This was the general situation when our troops arrived: a landed class dying of isolation and less and
less able to protect itself from the Navajo, and a tenant
class, and a poor but independent class full of resent-
ments and on the verge of revolt. As Kearny said, we
did not come to rob the Spanish Americans of their
property. Nonetheless, we have dispossessed a great
many of them. They were not businesslike; we were.
They ran up bills at the general stores, and lost their
property to merchants on mortgages. They liked the
idea of dams and conservancy of water, without realiz-
ing that they could not afford to pay the taxes such
improvements make necessary. They lost their land.
But even so they did not fully understand what they
were up against in Yankees and in lawyers. They still
do not understand. The Spanish American is said to
be a man of leisure and of pleasure, and so he is when
his circumstances permit it, at least compared to us.
We are hesitant about the uses of leisure and of
pleasure, if not really afraid of them. We are practical,
a race of workers, an acquisitive race.

What *we* did not understand was that the Spanish-
speaking people we were taking into our Union had
been living in the hermetically sealed Southwest for
three centuries, and so were not nineteenth-century
but sixteenth-century people, with the tools, the cus-

toms, and the point of view of a long distant age changed only enough to adapt them to survive in difficult natural surroundings. And even so Spain had had to make them concessions to insure their survival. She practically exempted them from taxes, and gave patronage to local and governmental services. Most of all she aided them by subsidies in the form of land grants. Originally made to individuals or to groups of heads of families, these grants soon became community property. In the earlier days all land was owned in common except home sites and farms. A council apportioned the grazing and water rights and saw to it that they were used equitably. The settlers worked together to dig the ditches and keep them open. Each landowner did his share on a basis of the amount of land he owned. This co-operative scheme of life even included the Indian villages when they used the same ditches. It was a pastoral age, a modified communalism, and it sufficed for the needs of the colony, which could neither import nor export goods, used barter instead of money, counted wealth in terms of herds.

Thus colonial life was not unlike that of the Indians of the region. The fact was not perceived by the U. S. Americans, nor was it recognized in the treaty of Guadalupe Hidalgo which gave us the territory. The Mexicans were a white race like ourselves and we extended the franchise to them, and all civil and religious liberties. Then, satisfied by recognizing them

as our equals, we went at them with our commercial
and competitive system of life and our high taxes.
And the first legislators for the new territory, though
almost entirely native and enacting their laws in Spanish, failed to insure for their own future and that of
their people a single guarantee or economic bulwark.

So from the economic view it has been like well-
armed people making war on those naked, or like
acquisitive adults coming among a race of children.
A few of the natives favored by situation and wealth
or by tremendous ability were able to jump three centuries ahead and meet us on our own terms. For the
great majority of rural settlers it has been tragedy
after tragedy. We have taken their communal lands
away from them, and thrust them back on little farms
which were never designed for more than the barest
subsistence agriculture, and then taxed the little farms.
The result today is that in the rural districts the natives are becoming more and more a people of migra-
tory workers. The effect of government relief is naturally to make an increasingly ominous number of
them public charges. The Spanish American forms
fifty-two per cent of the population. The first century
of democracy in the Southwest has been for the natives, I am afraid, a progressively horrible experience.

The source of hope lies in the spread among us of
the feeling that democracy cannot work of itself, that
we must make it work. We no longer think it means

anything to say, we are all free and equal, for we are not. We have already acted on this belief with the Pueblos and the Navajo. J. Francisco Chaves, Territorial Superintendent of Public Instruction, said in his report to the governor in 1901 referring to federal land grants made to New Mexico, "It was tardy justice indeed that brought to New Mexico the original grant. How small and niggardly it all appears now that we have witnessed what the federal government is doing for its newly acquired Porto Rican, Cuban and Philippine territory in the lavish expenditure of public moneys for the educational equipment of the masses."

Chaves was the first official to hit this nail on the head. I am glad he did not live to see the millions of dollars poured out upon the Navajo in the last few years, a fifth of which would have restored new hope and happiness to his own people. New awareness of democracy should teach us the need of a concerted approach to the land, health, tax, and educational problems of the natives. The federal government is growing aware of the injustice toward them. Only forty-two per cent of the area of the state is privately owned, as it happens. The government owns thirty-two million acres, the state thirteen million acres. So it is possible for the government, through the soil conservation service, to experiment with a policy of improving certain lands and administering them in the interests of the residents of an area. This is actually happening. It is only a beginning, but the institution of communal property may thus return to the native farmer. Like his fellows in Old Mexico he cannot exist on a few irrigable acres but must have elbow-room for grazing.

11. Nambe

Nambe, the only small rural community in the southwest with a full-time public health nurse under the supervision of the state health department, next month will observe the second anniversary of a health program that has benefited every class and family of the community.

—*New Mexico Capital-Examiner,* Santa Fe

WHEN you leave the highway and turn up the wide valley to Nambe (Nambay), you see mountains ahead, real mountains, the high peaks of the Sangres. In summer your eye lifts to the lush green flanks and bosoms of aspen and then above them to the bald heads of the giants. In winter the giants sleep under a blinding white cover, and at sunset the snow takes the imprint of cerise and violet. Most nights the year round the sky is near, a little above you. The stars hang their gold showers down, like flax its blue flowerets along a garden-walk in June. But if there has been a summer cloudburst in the mountains and vapor still hides the stars, you may feel lost in a world of white, and be a little fearful hearing the flood coming down the wash and rolling the boulders together.

The valley is humble and liveable. It is a great relief, whether you come from north or south. On either side, stretch miles of eroded land, upland pastures with no pasture, meadows with no harvest, brown pagodas or temples left by wind and storm. Then suddenly a wide wash, a trickle of water, and the world is again the world where man can live, consider his lot, make plans for his future, help his fellows and get help from them. You see something more than mountains. You see a community school with a full-time nurse, one of the four hundred and seventy in the whole country (for five out of six of our rural communities in the United States go without). You see a particular spot where meet and mingle the four great themes of southwestern life: exile, hardship, adaptation, and hope.

These four themes here and everywhere are pretty much the business of woman. In the United States, the richest of countries, a million families in 1935-1936 had an income of less than $21 a month, and the figure includes the estimated value of non-money farm income. There are 29,000,000 American families in all; a full half live on less than $96.50 a month. In a democracy statistics are a kind of compass to steer by—as are the stars. Some people can read both statistics and the stars, and that is good.

The Nambe women, the women of all these hill villages settled by the Spanish, have come through the centuries with much beauty and rightness in their lives. No doubt, like Núñez and his compadres, they thought it better to do the suffering themselves than to make others suffer. Their suffering has been intricate and a devastation. It is a long way back to Oñate and the first Spanish settlements. The problem of adaptation to life on the land in this new and remote country, instead of lessening for the settlers and their descendants, has steadily increased. Above all, in regard to the first necessity of their human adaptation, health. A community school attacks this particular phase of exile from the world of knowledge and helpful contemporary human relationship, never absent from any rural community, and acute in New Mexico.

Miss Marie Casias, the young nurse of Spanish descent, from Colorado and trained at Oberlin, allows me to read and quote from her journal (changing the names). This journal gives you a look into the recesses of a life of exile and ignorance, such as the native villages have known even during the century of United States government. Miss Casias, a conversable and charming young woman, talks frankly to her journal, and is full of solicitude:

"Saw Mrs. Ramón Villagrá today. She had a miscarriage, seems glad her pregnancy terminated. Has a year-old baby who is extremely malnourished. Child gets very little care, flies are eating the child up. . . .

"Our babies are still having diarrhea; too many flies in the homes.

"I keep talking about the proper location of toilets and wells. How to protect cribs and baby bottles from flies. How to tell if well is contaminated (empty two packages of salt in privy; if water in well tastes salty it is contaminated, not safe for anyone to drink). . . .

"People here do not seem to have grasped the meaning of venereal disease. They seem diseases that just happen to be contracted. Syphilis is just bad blood. . . .

"Started treatments on Baby Martinez. Child is in secondary stage of syphilis, pitiful. Can only tolerate very weak solution of milk. Mother knows nothing about baby care, is very stupid about following advice. Believes her neighbors more than she does the doctor or nurse.

"Baby Trujillo, baby with gonorrheal eyes, has been receiving treatment, is now much better. . . .

"Anselmo Sandoval has been sentenced to two years of prison. That means we will have that family back on our hands. . . .

"Called to see Amadeo Alarid's baby. Parents sure child has the evil eye. Temperature 102, abdomen distended, very restless, diarrhea. Prescribed treatment and explained to parents and grandparents that 'evil eye' is a condition known only to Spanish people. Hope they decide for themselves that it is a superstition. Mother of this baby very nervous, believes she has worms; believes they practically jump out of her mouth—has a mental picture of her anatomy as follows: Mouth—tube—stomach—one intestine—worm."

The natives live in their neat adobe houses along the highway, and back among the cottonwoods and green fields. It is a more fortunate village than most in respect to diet. More vegetables and fruits grow here than in most places. The natives can include peaches, apricots, and apples in their diet of beans, potatoes, and chili. The women are established in the custom of canning, and during August and September they can all the corn, carrots, string beans, and fruit possible. They make jams and jellies. The irrigable land averages only two acres to a family. Inheritance has divided and subdivided original holdings, wealthy out-of-state people have come in and purchased land for summer homes, and this dire situation is the result. Almost anywhere a farm should be twenty acres if it is to support a family of six. But in New Mexico soil conditions and water problems make thirty-five acres necessary. Here is the basic problem of a great proportion of rural natives today; they need help, and need it soon. During the summer whenever they can get the water the men and boys work day and night irrigating. The Indian pueblo of Nambe, being nearer to the watershed, has control of the supply. Unfortunately, the natives and the Pueblos are not bosom friends; the Indians have trouble sometimes about being generous.

The chief food deficiencies of the valley are milk and Vitamin C. If tomatoes grew here it would help correct malnutrition. The natives raise a good deal of cabbage, and cabbage is a source of Vitamin A. Beans furnish them with calcium and protein, and the protein takes care of the deficiency of meat diet. But Marie Casias hopes to give each child an orange daily, and the hope runs lyrically through her journal.

Many of the 147 families have no horses, cows, or sheep. They eke out their cultivation of small irrigated fields, by part-time seasonal employment elsewhere. Some receive government aid. The land would yield more if it were not badly eroded, and thus erosion becomes a matter of concern for the school. The idea is to develop the studies that meet community needs.

It was a thoughtful woman, Florence McCormick, who first had the idea of this community school. She and her husband, U. S. Americans, had come to live in the valley, and their thought and feeling had penetrated beneath the surface of the native people. They told County Superintendent Granito that they would help such a school if the university would supervise the program. This brought the guidance of Professor L. S. Tireman into the picture, and the group of four began to meet. They discovered that much could be

done; already in existence were the agencies prepared
to help drive ahead such an idea. Most of these agencies exist in every county, and what is happening in
Nambe could happen elsewhere, if the ability to co-
ordinate were less rare.

These agencies are so diverse it is well to list them:
The General Education Board, the State University,
the State Public Health Service and Vocational Departments, the County Health Department, the Agricultural Agent and Home Demonstration Agent, the
National Youth Administration, the WPA, the Soil
Conservation Service, the Forest Service, the Children's Bureau, the Department of Labor. One may
well wonder at the hodgepodge of agencies which had
to be utilized to secure a little service for a few children and families. But most older administrative units
having to do with schools are archaic. They date from
colonial and pioneer days when service was practicable
only on a local basis. Local units now vary enormously
in area and population. The average area of a Kentucky county is 334 square miles, of an Arizona county
8,129 miles. And of course there are counties in the
East that have a greater population than whole states
out West. The entire system needs to be rearranged,
together with the antiquated ideas of taxation that
support it. Those who have studied the humiliating situation today say that responsibility should rest with
the state to see to schooling, recreation, health, and

medical service; each state should make equalizing grants to localities, and the federal government should equalize the financial position of the states themselves by grants. It seems to make sense.

In New Mexico there is an astonishing disparity among the counties as regards school budgets and current expenses. For example, in 1938-39 Lea County, preponderantly U. S. American, had $2,974 a classroom unit, while Santa Fe County, a mixture, had $1,506, Taos County, preponderantly native, $887. The state law in force provides for a general state tax levy for common schools throughout the state, and the subsequent apportionment of the tax fund to counties on an equitable basis of school needs. So that the law would seem to be right, and the trouble doubtless lies in a misinterpretation of it to the wrongful injury of native counties. About eighty per cent of the current costs of public schools in the state are met from state sources, and this fact leads Professor George I. Sanchez to say, in his book, *Forgotten People,* "If Taos County received its pro rata share of state school funds it would have, from that source alone, more to spend for public schools than it does at present from both state and county sources." All our children are entitled to the same care, of course; none can be orphans or stepchildren. But only supervision by the federal government can make it happen. And the expenditure of

funds should be in the hands of trained workers se-
lected and retained on a merit basis.

So, in our present pioneer condition as regards the
care of children, all these timbers were lying about in
New Mexico waiting to be fitted together, and some
people at Nambe who wanted a community school fitted them together with the help of a wise university
professor, and made them of use. The animating idea
was that a school has to be the center of the community, awake to the needs, able to work with parents to
use available resources. "We shall try to find out what
is most needed in the lives of the people of this community and minister to that before all else."

The Nambe school has done pretty well in securing
adult co-operation, though naturally it did not come
all at once. Miss Casias says to her journal, "In my
home visits lately I notice a great change, people are
very friendly. At first they were at least courteous, now
they believe most of the things we tell them. Yesterday
I was talking about diet with a post-natal, and she said
she had never eaten fruit after delivery, but if I advised it she would eat it."

Parents and other adults form an Advisory Board,
and this board gave a dance to raise funds. Miss Casias
notes, "After all expenses were paid we had $45. All
the people of the community have co-operated well."
I read Miss Casias's journal more assiduously than the
journals of Opal Whitely or Marie Bashkirtseff, and I

like her care about money: "So many of our children have poor flabby gums. Saw Mr. Evans about toothbrushes. We can get them for eight cents apiece if we order a hundred. Children will be asked to pay for them."

Miss Casias is an angel. She thinks of money day and night. She knows what money means. Another entry: "Our advisory committee raised sixteen dollars for correction of defects. We hope this money will be matched by the state."

We all live on the new frontier of American life, the economic problem. We all know that sickness grows as we descend the economic scale and medical care declines. Which means that generally speaking health can be purchased. We all know that with lack of money, lack of work, it is hard to make family life secure; but that family life can be conserved, and children can be conserved, just as forests can, or the soil. And something else is growing clear, a truth everybody is getting an inkling of. President Hoover tried to summarize it when he said the world moves forward on the feet of little children.

There is a room full of cribs at this community school. I saw it one winter morning when all the cribs had babies in them, and embers glowed in the corner fireplace. There were all kinds of cribs, home-made, store-made; all kinds of coverlets—and the little room was so crammed I couldn't see how anyone could go in there to retrieve the babies. For the babies themselves it appeared to be time out from the exacting business of kindergarten. A few quiet black-haired brown-eyed faces took cognizance of my respectful stare. Seed for the future of the United States: a little room full of the future.

Miss Casias started a class for girls who had finished the eighth grade, and thirteen girls came to the first meeting, and they were allowed to ask the questions the answers to which would be the subject matter of the meeting. As I have Miss Casias's permission to do so, I copy the questions out of her journal for some of these meetings:

I

1. How can I develop personality?
2. How should I take care of my hair and complexion?
3. In what way is a city girl different from a country girl?
4. What is the cause of poor posture?
5. What will improve poise?
6. How should I take care of my feet?
7. Why do I get tired?
8. How can we be graceful?
9. Why do some people grow old prematurely?

Such questions concern people everywhere, if one can judge from the number of books published to answer them. But the second group was more drastic and fundamental.

II

1. How should I take care of myself during menstruation?
2. What should I know about marriage before getting married?
3. Is it true that a person can be half male and half female?
4. Why are babies born before it is time for them to be born?
5. Can a little girl five years old have a baby?
6. What should I know about pregnancy?
7. Why is there such a thing as love?
8. What are venereal diseases?
9. What are female diseases?
10. How can a girl regulate the size of her family?

Later Miss Casias notes, "Questions the girls have been asking have to do with personal hygiene and sex. They have had much misleading information and I am happy they are getting authentic facts."

I must have been surprised when I read these questions, for I can still see them in Miss Casias's handwrriting on the pages of her journal. Science may have gained information in regard to certain of them, but as a whole they deal with matters people have always known. If these girls of the hills did not know the answers, their traditional culture was breaking down under the strain of native life today. In the surprise that pressed my optic nerve was also the wondering: What must life be like for these girls until they can get their questions correctly answered? It was not hard to see fear, bewilderment, anxiety; depths of silence where there should be frankness.

Various women came to talk to this class. Miss Hester Jones of Santa Fe told Miss Casias about a summer course she had taken at her alma mater, Vassar. Possibly as a result of that talk the Nambe school had a kind of euthenics course. Euthenics is apparently the science of bettering living conditions to help human beings thrive. (The Greek source-word means "to thrive.") At the end of the course the girls were given questions to answer. Here are a few, which picture what the school may be doing for the young women of the valley:

Is it true that to have a child obey you is sometimes a great convenience to adults, whatever it may be to the child?

What are Sunday manners?

Does gossiping help develop personality?

Is it wise to raise children to believe that they are little kings and queens?

Is it wise to spend much money on a wedding outfit?

Is it possible to furnish a house attractively on little
money?

What method of birth control does the Catholic
Church sanction?

Parents should be companions to their children and
not owners to be feared—is that statement correct?

The girls were given also those other questions to
answer which come up every day of the year in all
rural communities—questions as usual as the wind, and
like the wind often bracing and cold and sometimes
bearing death.

What are the prime offenders in the distribution of
germs?

Mention one of the most common breeding places
of flies.

Name two important preventive measures against
rickets.

Twenty girls took this course. "They have been
faithful about coming. They are all bright girls."

What is exciting to think about is that the girls at
the Nambe school are going to live this new knowledge. It will become in them part of those modesties
and that need to cherish which kept their mothers
through the dark generations close to life and beautiful. Meaning controls everything in our lives, for every-

thing appears to respond to our attitude towards it, to the meaning we give it. It was their attitude that helped the mothers of these children endure their lot. Even when the institutions supposed to guide them proved useless, the blood of their own mothers guided them secretly, and their childhood memories. At least something guided them, something important to know about, and what else could it have been? Love is itself a religion; as Kagawa says, faith means a realization that one is loved, that love for one is hidden away at the heart of the universe, that somebody, something loves you, never wishes you broken and withered.

But sex is so elemental in our lives that to be handicapped in knowledge of it might mean loneliness or bereavement or death or insanity, as well as those endless illnesses which keep a woman fatigued and unable to cope with the demands her life as giver and nourisher lay upon her. Knowledge of sex, like all true knowledge of ourselves, is a great boon; it clarifies our path and trains our desire to cherish others. Knowledge of diet is not a whit less important. On it hang the issues of life or death for children, to say nothing of the issues of "rheumatism" for men and women who should be in their prime and are not. And by these concerns, which draw old and young together and unite family to family, a community school makes a group aware of its common problems and responsibilities.

12. *Agustin Huerta*

Yesterday, on the eve of another decade of advancing civilization, Agustin Huerta was bound over for preliminary hearing, January 8, before Justice of the Peace Carlos Barron on charges of witchcraft as the result of the mutilation of two woman members of his family. . . . Bond was set at $1,000. . . . It was estimated that 1,500 persons attended court or stood outside the courthouse. . . .

—A New Mexico newspaper

THE JUSTICE of the peace probably held Huerta on a charge of mayhem. New Mexico, being a tricultural state, has many curious laws; but witchcraft is not defined as a crime in the statutes, so far as I have heard. As Marie Casias said, witchcraft is a condition known chiefly to the Spanish people.

Mrs. Huerta, who signed the complaint, told the justice that her husband Agustin had bewitched her and her daughter, and her daughter's husband, Vicente F. Chacon. She had quarreled with Agustin a few days before, and he had left the house. When he returned he traced a cabalistic design on the floor with his feet, snapped his fingers in the face of each of the three, and departed as the clock struck seven.

That night the three adults, with the Chacon children aged fourteen and five, barred the doors and windows. Soon afterward they heard somebody trying to get in. They peered out, but could see no one, and there were no tracks on the new-fallen snow. Mrs. Huerta testified that between ten and eleven that night she was wakened by a scream. Chacon awakened also. He turned up an oil lamp, and the light revealed a huge toad with a long tail near the window. He grabbed a shovel and threw it at the toad. The toad jumped in the direction of the bed formerly occupied by Mrs. Huerta's son, who had died a few weeks before. Then it disappeared.

They were all terrified, they said, but went back to sleep and slept soundly till morning. When they awoke the two women, who were sleeping together, found themselves somewhat the worse for wear. Fingers on both Mrs. Huerta's hands were lacerated to the bone in wounds caused by human teeth, and two of Mrs. Chacon's front teeth were missing. Both women looked as though their faces had been chewed.

These incidents occurred at a settlement of fourteen persons a few miles north of the county seat, at the entrance to a forbidding canyon. It is a remote region, and seven murders have occurred in the canyon within three years. The women opened the door Christmas morning to go to town to file charges against Agustin. In the fresh snow by the doorstep was a hexing design, a crossed circle. Tracks like a cat's appeared within the circle, but none led to or from it.

In the courtroom the women would not look at Agustin, nor would he look at them. Mrs. Huerta, testifying further regarding her husband's supernatural powers, said that a week before she had threatened to shoot him with a rifle during a quarrel. He had only laughed at her and said, "Go ahead." She found herself powerless to pull the trigger.

Agustin, who stands about five feet and weighs one hundred pounds, smiled and denied his wife's charges. At first the justice held him in $3,000 bail. He reconsidered the amount and reduced it to $1,000. Agustin was able to post it without much difficulty, though it would be a great sum in those parts. While preliminary hearing had been set for January 8, the district attorney indicated that the state was prepared to accept a physician's analysis of the evidence, and would drop the case unless new evidence came to light. He said it was useless to "prosecute Huerta on any charges when the complaining witnesses were ready to swear it was impossible for him to have entered the room."

The physician in question said the affair looked to him like this: "Mrs. Huerta, possibly during a nightmare, stuck her hand in Mrs. Chacon's mouth. The latter then bit into her fingers, and Mrs. Huerta naturally struck and scratched to break loose. When she jerked her hand out of Mrs. Chacon's mouth, two teeth came with it. Mrs. Chacon had an advanced case of pyorrhea and it was no trick to dislodge the teeth. Mrs. Chacon showed me the teeth when she came for treatment."

Agustin is the type of man whose independence of spirit results in his being gossiped about and feared. Such persons have from time immemorial been martyrs to some darkness inside of us. Agustin had worked on every WPA job in the vicinity for six or seven years, and was first regarded as a brujo (witch) by his fellow workers. Suspicion fastened on him for the reason that he was a light sleeper.

"No matter how late the last one went to bed at those WPA camps," I was told, "Agustin was never seen to go to bed. No matter how early the earliest of them got up, he would find Agustin ahead of him, with the fire going. They said they had looked into Agustin's tent in the middle of the night, but they never saw him in bed."

Agustin has a prepossessing face. His expression is quizzical, as though he had his own opinion of the human race, and not a flattering one. But it is an honest face, with a determination in it to live his life the way he pleases to. Unfortunately for his local reputation, one of his eyes has a slight misalignment. It is hard to know whether he is looking at you or just beyond you.

Justice Barron has known Agustin for thirty years. "He always seemed a very insignificant man until recently," said the Justice. When he first knew him, Agustin was working for the biggest sheep outfit in Montana.

"He was getting fifty dollars a month, working under an uncle who was foreman. This uncle used to take Agustin's salary and squander it. He did this for years. Then one day when this big sheep company was sold, the owners found how the uncle had been cheating Agustin, and they gave him a check for three thousand dollars. It is quite possible that he still has most of this money saved up."

Agustin leads a lonely life, rarely if ever joining the Saturday crowd at the county seat. His thrift is regarded as miserliness, and many people believe he has large sums of money buried at his home. The officers who arrested him found five pocketbooks, and a tobacco sack stuffed with $115 in currency. They also found $350 more in cash.

In the democratic poverty of mountain life, such details make the picture of a human being dangerous because different. Let us sum them up. Agustin is always working. He has a good deal of money and many pocketbooks. He prefers to stay by himself. He has been seen walking round at night. He has never been seen asleep in bed. When he looks at you you can't be sure he is really looking at you. His smile has something strange in it, as though he had you sized up. He has no fear, and if you want to shoot him he says, go ahead, and you can't pull the trigger.

So Agustin is someone to think about. There he is today up in the mountain fastnesses, a marked man. In all directions from that region the day, the night are limitless, and no house is protection against the illimitable even if a crucifix in the corner does catch the firelight. And few minds are protection against it; in those inward abysses of human consciousness terrors from the beginning of time still lurk, ready to lunge forward the moment common sense and the feeling of human affection are relaxed. The lean sinewy form of Agustin goes through the trees and along the roads; superstitions are merely cobwebs to him, and he brushes them aside easily. But the loneliness of the man whose tastes and thoughts are of a different order from his fellows is no superstition. Let us hope that Agustin knows a few people, little children perhaps, with whom he can share a joy or two.

13. Marijuana

José Z. Baca, Plaza Vigil, was charged today with possession of marijuana, in a complaint filed in district court. Baca was arrested Tuesday night by City Policeman Martinez Romero, called to investigate a disturbance at the Baca home.

—A New Mexico newspaper

A DISTURBANCE at the Baca home" is just such a vague phrase as marijuana always breeds. It is a drug which introduces what is unforeseeable or unaccountable into situations. Five years ago the federal government charged a Pueblo Indian named Telesfor Vigil with the murder of a fellow Indian, a friend of his at the same pueblo, named Yndelecio Torres. Murders among Pueblos are very rare, and this case never came to trial through a legal technicality. Detective William Martin of Santa Fe in his investigation found both liquor and marijuana to be involved, but the impression you have from Martin's examination of Vigil is chiefly of marijuana:

"Q. Before this tragedy you and Yndelecio did some quarreling. Please tell us about the first occasion."

"A. He was living at my house with me and my

122

brother. We were doing the best we can for him, but he made all kinds of trouble so we had to put him out of the house. This was the first trouble. . . .

"The second trouble was one time as I was coming from the pueblo and he met me and wanted to fight. I did not pay any attention to him. . . ."

"Q. On the night of November 12, when Yndelecio came and knocked at your door, you let him in?"

"A. Yes. He was very nice and spoke to me very politely, and said, 'How are you, my friend,' and I answered him, 'Very well, thank you.' And when we were getting ready to go to bed then is when the argument started. . . ."

"Q. Who started the argument? Tell us the truth about that."

"A. He started the argument, Yndelecio. He told me, 'I have a very bad feeling against you and I am going to fight it out. . . .' Then I told him, 'You have to get out or go to bed.'"

"Q. Then what did you do?"

"A. I asked him again if he was going to get out and he refused, and then I got hold of this club."

Both Yndelecio and Telesfor had been drinking liquor. To give or sell liquor to an Indian is a federal offense. They had obtained it from Spanish American bootleggers near the pueblo, who were afterwards prosecuted and jailed. They were old friends, and there seems no intelligible reason for the quarrels.

When Yndelecio came to Telesfor's house he was friendly and polite; a moment later he had a bad feeling towards Telesfor and proposed to fight it out, whatever "it" was. This is the way marijuana works, producing violent changes of mood, then terrible happenings.

Unlike peyote, the hempweed grows or can grow anywhere in the United States. It is the cheapest of evil drugs, the hardest to control. It has been found growing in the prison yard at Alcatraz. The federal narcotics bureau and the police of the different states are agreed that it is extraordinarily vicious. Officers are wary in approaching a marijuana smoker, whether child or man; they know he is apt to kill without warning. If chemists and laboratory workers view the weed through rosier spectacles, it is that they do not see it in action. And if literature contains delightful accounts of marijuana dreams, it may be that in the countries where it is known as hasheesh it acts differently upon the human organism.

Detective Martin's reputation in the little-populated parts of northern New Mexico did wonders in maintaining law and order when he was on the force. He kept alive the tradition of courage and pertinacity the country has bred in the past. He deserves a biographer. But his biographer should be acquainted with modern criminology so that he can see Martin as the adept he is. A man now of about forty-five, he is a Swiss by birth. Three of his uncles were chiefs of police in Switzerland, and one was head of the secret service there for a time. Martin came to Canada as a boy and was trained in the Mounties. Before we entered the World War he was in the U. S. intelligence service in France. He has been in the Southwest eighteen years, and in that time has handled one hundred and seventy-four murder cases and had only one defeat in open court. He has never killed a man.

Some years since, Martin was called to a Spanish American village about thirty-five miles north of Santa Fe. Five men, all friends, had left the dance hall together the night before, but one of them never reached home. He was found lying in a ditch by the road, pretty much cut up but still alive. Martin carries a first-aid kit. After he had taken the four men into custody, he went to work to save the fifth. This man had suffered three deep wounds in the stomach, among others, and the detective found he could do nothing about them. He put his prisoners into his car, and with the three men in the rear seat holding the wounded man across their knees, drove back to Santa Fe to the hospital.

That night the sick man's condition seemed hopeless, and a doctor telephoned Martin he had better come if he wished a confession. So Martin came, with a stenographer. It was about two in the morning, and one could hear a pin drop in the hospital.

"How do you feel?" he asked the man.

"Muy malo, amigo," in a big sighing voice.

"Now look. If you're going to get well, I don't want to bother you. But if you're going to die, you've got to tell me what happened. Are you going to get well, or not?"

Martin waited two minutes before the answer came, in the same big voice.

"My frien' Detecteévo Marteén, me going to tell you somethin'. Me no feel good, me no feel bad. My heart she sad, but Jesu' Christ my stomach she hurt like hell."

The voice rolled down the corridors, and two Sisters giggled at the far end. That ended the attempt to get a death-bed confession.

Martin had noticed that the man smelt of marijuana as he lay in the ditch. The detective tried to get the story from him the three weeks he was in the hospital. He would not talk. When he was well, Martin put him in the city jail and threatened to send him to the penitentiary for having marijuana on his person. The threat started him talking. He had little to say, but what he said was enough, and it came down to the fact that he had no knowledge at all of what had happened. On the night in question the five friends were walking along in the moonlight having a quiet talk and a quiet smoke of marijuana, and he suddenly grew sleepy and lay down to take a nap. He slept so soundly and the drug was such a good anesthetic that he felt no pain when his friends, from some whim bred of marijuana, fell on him with their knives. And his friends, when *they* came to, had had no recollection either of their uninhibited moments the night before.

Baudelaire, Bayard Taylor, Ludlow, and others record beautiful dreams under the influence of hasheesh; this story of William Martin's shows the way the drug worked on a road near Chimayo one night.

I said to Martin, "Is marijuana as responsible for crime as whiskey?"

"More responsible," was his instant reply; and he continued, "I have had case after case in which marijuana appears. So once I thought I'd try it myself. I went up into the mountains where nobody was near that I could hurt. I smoked a part of a cigarette. When the effect hit me it was beyond anything I expected: I felt like a giant [Martin stands about five feet five and is slender]; I had to keep myself from tearing up the forest around there."

He told me another marijuana story, about a big dance given at a marriage in another mountain community. Three hundred people were there, but no one was killed. It is unique in Martin's experience of big dances in the remote districts. When he approached the door (I believe the parents of the young couple had asked him to come), he smelt the gray sweetish smell of marijuana. "Oh-ho," he thought. He began searching

the men and taking their guns away from them. When
a man resisted he knocked him out and told his friends
to lug him home. In a place like this one there would
be no jail, and of course no hospital. After a while it
seemed useless to go on confiscating dozens of guns
he couldn't keep track of. Tear-gas seemed the better
way, and he had a few shells of it in his pocket. He
removed the caps and went among the dancers dropping the powder on the floor. Their feet ground down
on it and pretty soon the fumes began to rise. Martin
hazarded the guess to the orchestra that they were
playing the last piece they would play that evening.
They soon agreed with him; in five minutes the baile
was deserted. Nobody was dead or maimed, the officer
of the law had outwitted marijuana.

The chemical constitution of marijuana has been
endlessly investigated, without final conclusions. In his
study, *Marijuana, America's New Drug Problem,* Professor Robert P. Walton of the University of Mississippi considers full success doubtful until there is a co-
ordinated program of investigation in which chemical
alterations can be guided directly by accurate meas-
urements of physiologic activity. The Cambridge
chemists Wood, Spivey, and Easterfield obtained a relatively active product by vacuum distillation of some
of the more potent extracts, and first used the term

"Cannabinol." It is not an alkaloid; certain chemists think it may be a tertiary alcohol.

Incidentally, the Cambridge chemists were pursued by a series of tragedies. Easterfield was killed in an explosion while attempting to hydrogenate cannabinol. Spivey lost his life in a synthetic study of nitro-cannabinolactone, and Wood escaped by the skin of his teeth when he took some cannabinol at the time he was preparing zinc ethyl. Even in the laboratory and to the scientific technician marijuana is a drug dangerous out of the ordinary.

14 This Business of Pardons

New Mexico's stringent capital punishment laws, unexecuted since 1933, will remain impotent for another two years, Gov. John Miles indicated last week, as he lifted the death penalty from a nineteen-year-old boy who confessed to marching an old man into a lonely draw in southern New Mexico and shooting him to death in cold blood because he could not produce a ransom.

Governor Miles followed the practice set by Gov. Clyde Tingley in using the power of his office to supersede sentences of the courts. . . . —A New Mexico newspaper, 1938

B UT BEFORE Tingley Governor Seligman exercised his constitutional right to override the action of the courts, through commutation of sentence, pardon, and parole; and the practice is political and of long standing.

Some of these crimes for which people are pardoned are quite interesting, if you can be as detached from them as a New Mexico governor. One of Seligman's pardons went to the man in the screen-door murder case. William Martin told me the story. I wish he might have told it to Maupassant; it would appeal to the author of *A Piece of String*. The scene was one of those weather-worn villages under the high peaks, where summer is short and winter enduring, and things small in themselves assume grotesque importance in the monotony of village life.

A native who lived in this village decided to make himself a screen door. There was much talk, and the man and his wife were in a dither about it, and some of the neighbors were jealous that they should even have so ambitious an idea. The man came to town to find out how much the materials would cost. He was shown a ready-made door at the lumber yard, which somebody had ordered but never taken. It was even painted, and a suitable green. It was the right size, and it only cost him $1.98. He took this prize home and put it on his front door the same evening. He boasted about it the next few days, and his next-door neighbor made up his mind to kill him. Troublesome boasters are bound to cause homicidal impulses in every rank of society; these impulses are natural enough, if they are passing. But it was no passing fancy on the part of the neighbor. Martin discovered later that the man looked up the murder laws, and even consulted a justice of the peace. He wanted to make sure that if you took marijuana first, you could not be convicted of first-degree murder. The justice of the peace told him that such was his understanding of the law, but he added that he wasn't sure "what Bill Marteén would think." Martin, by showing that the murder was premeditated and the marijuana a blind, as a matter of fact secured a conviction of first-degree murder in this case. The prisoner had served several years of a life-sentence when the governor pardoned him.

The actual state of lawlessness in the Southwest is not featured in books on the region; it would not be conducive to the tourist's peace of mind. Besides, it is difficult to go into it because of native psychology. No evildoer likes to be reminded of his prison record; the Spanish American evildoer will resent it to the point of taking some action. Let us suppose that such a man murders his wife and goes to the penitentiary and in several years obtains a pardon. He considers he has paid his debt to society for what was an incident of his private life. He does not regard himself as an ex-convict, and to refer to him as one and mention him by name is to invite trouble. Family, lawyers, friends, fellow members of secret societies, who got him out of the penitentiary, are still at his disposal to wipe out an insult. Because of the great many natives with similar names the newspapers have to be careful. You often see such an item as this, "The Antonio Y. Roybal who was reported yesterday as arrested for drunkenness is not the Antonio Y. Roybal who lives on Cisneros Street."

Enforcement of the law is not easy in a county like Rio Arriba, perennially without money to prosecute criminals. A trial is a luxury bankrupt communities must forego. The judge, the jury, the police, must all be fed, lodged, transported, and paid. Few Americans have any idea of how expensive crime is, or of the very great proportion of their tax money that goes to its prevention and punishment. It is one of the subjects high-school and college students are not instructed in hour after hour, day after day. Such advisable instruction is prevented by the magical nature of our system of education.

Spanish Americans in the outlying districts grow fatalistic. They see no earthly help for their afflictions, and so they submit to them. Dr. Albert W. Egenhofer of the Proctor Eye Clinic once remarked to me that his patients often set their troubles down to their destiny, or even to the wish of the Invisible.

Thus natives will submit patiently to the depredations of terrorizing gangs. In five years of the middle 1930's a gang of night-riders inflicted more than $100,-000 damage on the merchants, farmers, and property owners in various parts of Rio Arriba County. They burned the post office at Canjilón, the Sargent-Martin store at El Rito, haystacks in many a field, barns sometimes filled with horses and cattle. And the poor people who suffered such depredations kept still about it, for fear that if they complained worse things might befall them. The night-riders were captured and sent to the penitentiary. Some have been pardoned, some served out their sentences. And from the newspaper accounts they, or another gang like them, are today riding Rio Arriba County again.

A spoils system of government produces odd incidents. Some years ago when Martin had occasion to arrest a young native for matricide, of a powerful family two of whose members were already in the penitentiary, the governor at the moment exclaimed (so the story went), "Martin has gone too far this time!"

In addition to the night-riders, Rio Arriba County in the 1930's also had a gang of robbers. Martin ran them down, all of them, and that he could do so was due to the fact that a small group of U. S. Americans put up the money the county lacked. The riders made a mistake in robbing these persons, for their indifference to general conditions in Rio Arriba vanished the moment they themselves were victimized. The U. S. American when robbed does not for a moment consider it the will of God. Rather, he considers it the will of God that he should put the robber in jail as soon as possible. This attitude makes it easier to enforce the law.

Martin will have to tell the story himself some day, but there is one incident I intend to preserve myself. At the beginning of his search for the gang, he encountered the leader himself at a flooded arroyo near Española. He was not ready to arrest the man as yet.

Martin's Ford was the first car to be halted by the flood; the gangster stopped his Studebaker behind him and got out. He was a big man with a red kerchief round his throat, high boots, blue woolen shirt. He walked up to the Ford and recognized Martin with surprise and displeasure, but with a sweep of his arm toward the mountains, remarked, "Grand country, ain't it?"

Martin answered, "Ain't it? When I wake up in the morning and see the sun and hear the meadow lark, and go out in the yard and see the mountains shining, I feel mighty sorry for people who could have enjoyed all this if they had done right."

The other considered this point of view.

"I tell you what, Martin," he said, "if you want to go on seeing the sun and hearing the meadow lark and watching the grass grow, you lay off me. If you don't, it's going to be too bad for you."

Martin in turn reflected. "If you stop me from waking up in the morning and seeing the grass grow and hearing the meadow lark, what will happen to you? You won't have a chance. Before you know it you'll be sitting in the chair."

Red with rage the robber spun round and strode back to his Studebaker. As soon as the flood subsided he crossed after Martin, and roared past him down the road.

The western meadow lark, the "prairie lark," is dear not only to detectives and criminals, but to everyone who has ears to hear it. The youthful Mozart said to his sister, of a composition he was working on, "Remind me to put in something good for the horn." No writer on the Southwest would need to be reminded to put in something good for the prairie lark. Harvey Fergusson speaks of its "high clear bugle" that "comes nearer than any other bird to making of real music." Thomas Hornsby Ferril has a line in a poem, "The prairies melt into the throats of larks."

The lark is a bird you don't often see but can hear on highways from British Columbia all the way south to Jalisco. It will nest in the hottest valleys, like Carlsbad, and up to 8,000 feet on the Mesilla mountains. What it likes best is open country and water, and approaching a water tank or a water hole you are almost sure to hear its song. In the Rio Grande valley you can hear it all winter, at least as far north as Española. The lark is the color of the ground, and nests on the ground. Its tail has a white border with broken markings on it and on the back, and its breast, which you hardly ever see, is golden with a jet black necklace. The mocking bird spends hour upon hour trying to capture the lark's song. He is consumed by a supreme passion to capture it, and now and then he succeeds even to the marvelous finale.

Once in the outskirts of Santa Fe I heard the lark at

sunset on the shortest day of the year, the ground under a foot of snow, and the temperature below zero. No bird can approach it for brightness and joy. The Southwest has unparalleled vistas of mesa, cloud, and mountain, but the lark is its chief beauty, and the beauty that unifies all.

I remember going out to Cienega with Lauro de Bosis, the Italian poet, who was shot down about 1934 while dropping anti-Fascist leaflets on Rome. He had never heard the lark before, and we talked about it and about the nightingale. His joy in the lark was great, but the song of the nightingale was dearer to him. "The lark has no death in his throat," he said. That is true, but I find it a reason for preferring the lark. There is no lack of death in the world, and it is good to have one supreme song that absorbs the shadows in a paean of joy.

15. Bronson Cutting

Bronson M. Cutting, U. S. Senator from New Mexico, was
killed early this morning in the crash of a transport plane. . . .

—*Kansas City Star,* May 6, 1935

I HAVE heard admirers of Bronson Cutting say that
if he had lived he would have been the Republican
nominee for President in 1940. Such remarks are to be
taken no doubt as expressions of hero-worship, but
they bring up an idea interesting to consider. If two
sets of circumstances had been in his favor (over one
of which he had control), Cutting might well have
been eligible for the presidential race. As to the first,
let us suppose that when he first came out here a sick
boy, or even later when he returned to Santa Fe from
his position of attaché at the London embassy during
the World War, he had begun to give concrete form to
that deep sympathy with the native New Mexicans
which he undoubtedly felt, had studied in detail their
tragedy as a group, and helped by the research of
trained investigators had drawn up a workable program of land and water recovery, had secured congres-

sional support for it and started it off upon a merciful career. It would need to be a federal matter because of the sharp conflict in property rights and interests it would entail; it would fall into line with governmental policies toward the Pueblo and the Navajo. And it was not at all beyond Cutting's power to start the ball rolling, for his prestige was great.

Let us suppose all this. And then let us suppose that in the course of international events the moment had arrived—as it now has—when it is vital for our national safety to be genuine friends with our Latin neighbors to the south. In this emergency nothing could stand us in better stead than to have a leader who had intelligently approached typical Latin problems in the one part of our country where they touch and affect us. It may be like saying that if a man had ham and got eggs he could have ham and eggs. But it seems to me that a great Destiny came near twitching Cutting's sleeve.

In the beginning Cutting was avid for details of native economy, so I have heard; he even had the idea of initiating in New Mexico a movement to better the conditions of the people on whom more and more he was to depend for power. But even for a senator, a day has only twenty-four hours. You cannot be in Washington and in Santa Fe at the same time. Cutting's record in Washington is one in which many of his constituents take justifiable pride. But in New Mexico he seemed engulfed, as do his successor Dennis Chavez and the rest of the politicians, in the morass of state politics. And for all his ability he remains, I am afraid, a somewhat ineffectual friend to the native.

People say that New Mexico politics is hard to understand. Surely this is to exaggerate. The peculiar political situation is extremely simple; you can understand it after you have been here a week. The difficulty lies in following the many changes in the picture: for example, with what power group is X now aligned, and why? There seems no rhyme or reason for the antagonisms or alliances, for none of the issues involved is particularly significant.

The politician who thinks of a way really to help the native people grow and find their rightful place in the American pattern will be New Mexico's first statesman.

The key to the situation is that generally speaking the rural natives, because of their lack of land and water, are at a disadvantage in becoming good Americans. Sometimes you are sick and you don't know why you are sick. Thus it is that rural natives do not understand the reasons for their trouble. Not knowing the reasons they do not stick together and fight for a common objective; in their ignorance they often defeat their friends and support their enemies. As a result they are fodder for partisan political machines and the spoils system. Election issues are intensely partisan, but have nothing much to do with problems vital to the majority of the electorate. The voters vote the Re-

publican or the Democratic ticket, with an eye to state
and local politics, not with an eye to which candidates
mean business in reforming the situation as to land,
labor, health, and education. The natives are involved
in politics, since it affects their day-to-day existence
and supply of money; yet civically, they are backward
and uninformed.

The result is not surprising—the counties prepon-
derately native furnish for themselves municipal and
county government so inefficient that it is hard to believe. In Taos County the native constitutes ninety per
cent of the population, and of this ninety per cent few
are in business or the professions. And so the part of
the county least experienced, least aware, least able to
rule well, elects the officials and dictates the policies.
Such is rather the state of affairs in from eight to fifteen counties, poetic retribution upon the settlers from
the states who are concerned. It will continue until
the citizens awake to the seriousness of a handicap
upon one sector of the community so serious that it has
already damaged thousands of people irretrievably.

Cutting seemed to me an intellectual of the intui-
tional type, and I judged his success due in part to his
taking over from the earlier and simpler society of colonial days the powerful pattern of the patrón. The natives do not forget the image of the patrón, the man
for whom they worked, who promised them protection, and to whom they went for help in any and every

emergency. A native acquaintance once told me that one day Cutting happened to stand behind him in line at a post-office window, and they began talking. He told the senator he was going to be married. Cutting congratulated him and he said, "If I thought you'd come to my wedding, I'd invite you." "Why wouldn't I come? I'd be your best man if you wanted me to," Cutting replied. "You'd never do that," exclaimed the incredulous native. But as it turned out the senator did stand up with him at the altar, and incidentally gave him a marriage gift of, I believe, $2,500.

Cutting was unstinting in his generosity with money at critical times in the ordinary native's hard-pressed life. He paid for many a funeral. He forged himself a personal weapon out of his Spanish American following so strong that he could be an independent in politics and change his party affiliation at will. He was wealthy, and from an old and established New York family. I have heard that he was despondent when he first came out here to regain his health. On this account his physician was not optimistic about his recovery. But he was induced to buy the *Santa Fe New Mexican,* the oldest newspaper in the state, and thus little by little he became engrossed in the ins and outs of state politics. Politics proved a congenial field and led little by little to his recovery. I have heard him called an aristocrat in the service of the people. This is to use words without meaning. If you serve the peo-

ple you are a democrat, and I would call Cutting a be-
lieving democrat.

He was a bachelor and a solitary figure. In the evening he enjoyed playing his player piano. He had a
group of friends and protégés living with him generally, and still he could hardly be called an accessible
or friendly person. I have seen him dozens of times
walking home from the newspaper office, reading the
paper as he walked and looking neither to right nor
left. He had little sense of humor, and was the last person to know how to escape when a native woman,
temporarily deranged, stopped him on the public
street and harangued him on the terrors of the grand
climacteric.

Whatever his stature as a political figure, Cutting as
a private person touches a chord in all of us. Surely
the zest of life, like the zest of a game, does not come
from having everything your own way. It comes from
the limitations life imposes on you, from understanding them and working within them. It is true that he
had wealth, but since when is wealth better than
health? For years the spark of life in him was uncertain. Whether it would blaze up or go out no one could
be sure. And he knew also the torture of extreme shy-
ness, his nature was reticent and veiled and introspec-
tive. A bookish fellow, it was hard for him to reach out
to people. But it is hard to believe that life is against

any of us, what matter how we are conditioned. It has its pitfalls, and terrors; yet the real foes to be overcome are lurking in ourselves—the apathy and the selfishness that prevent our accepting our fate. Cutting conquered his inward foes. And when he grasped power, it was not to him an end in itself, but so far as he could, being necessarily a politician, he used it as a weapon for the defenseless.

Bronson Cutting and I were classmates at Harvard, and thus it chanced that I introduced the speakers at the ceremonies for the unveiling of his bust on the grounds of the state capitol in Santa Fe. The cost of this monument was met by contributions from all counties of the state, and not one contribution had been solicited. Among the several hundred people who came that day many had driven hundreds of miles to do so. It seemed to me particularly fitting that Professor George Sanchez was one of the speakers. He came from the state university to pay a crisp and unsentimental tribute in Spanish to the senator. Sanchez was at the time engaged upon his work *Forgotten People,* a scientific survey of Taos County showing the life of the natives in a typical native community and indicating what may be done to better it—a pioneering study of signal value made possible by the Carnegie Corporation. A scientific approach is essential, yet sympathy for the natives must go with it; and Cutting more

than any other figure manifested that sympathy.
Hence his detractors say there was never a race question in the state till Cutting came. The question is not
of race, however, but of human misfortune.

16. Carson

Kit Carson III, grandson of the famed Indian scout, failed to win his first political race. He ran for Conejos county commissioner but was scalped by Juan Medina, who piled up a lead of more than 500 votes.

—*The Rocky Mountain Herald*, Denver, Colorado

I T IS too bad that Kit the third was scalped at the polls, but it is characteristic that he should be running for office. The original Kit, as soon as American civilization caught up with him, fitted into it as an excellent citizen, maybe the best of his time out here. His grave in the out-of-the-way but impressive little graveyard in Taos suggests solid burgherly qualities. There he lies with his native wife beside him, a big gravestone on him, a little one on her, and an iron fence about them. Near-by, inside wooden palings painted white, is the grave of Kit the second.

Garth Cate of the *New York World-Telegram* said to me, "When I'm in Santa Fe I always take an early morning walk to see the Kit Carson monument by the Federal Building. It has the finest inscription I ever saw, just four words, 'He led the way.'" Those four

146

words allude doubtless to Carson's being one of the first U. S. Americans to enter the Southwest. But it has a deeper meaning, in that he led the way in adaptation. The thoroughness and alacrity with which he could fit himself into the covered-wagon era, the period of the beaver trappers, that of the Indian wars, of the Mexican troubles, and of the final coming of law and order U. S. style, gives him the fascination of pliant yet obstinate souls who remain themselves under violently difficult conditions.

Carson came west so early in his life that he literally grew up with the country. At first he went wild with it; but the older men who befriended him and the Mexican girls and women of Taos who gave him food, taught him how to cook, and how to speak Spanish, adjusted the balance between one way of life and the other. Thus he had no underlying dislike of either, none of that sense of inability to fit in back East which characterized many of the mountain men and traders, and gave them the drive to go West and stay. All many of them achieved was an unhappy blending of two kinds of lives. Kit was lucky to see the good in each. He knew nothing of the economic, religious, or sexual cramping, and dinner daily at six-thirty, which his neurotic seniors had found unendurable in their homes to the East.

The interplay of the forces of civilization and those of the wilderness, and the excellent thing it is for a

man if he can keep those forces in balance since they
correct one another, was an idea a good deal in the
conversation of the late Langdon Mitchell, playwright
and author of *The New York Idea,* who spent his last
six or eight summers in the Southwest. I can hear his
resonant voice, see his white mustache, and red-
bronze cheeks. He was the son of S. Weir Mitchell
of Philadelphia, and as a boy he canoed down to Cam-
den to call on Walt Whitman. He was educated in
England and Germany, but half of his long life he
had spent in the out-of-doors and on the frontiers of
civilization. He was always talking about Washington
and Lincoln. One could rouse him by bringing him an
inept passage in a book or a speech, such as "Lincoln
had everything against him. His early environment
was one of squalor. In his sordid, narrow and stupefy-
ing surroundings there was nothing to aid him in his
effort to rise." Or, "Washington had no education. His
education was totally inadequate. He was never a cul-
tivated man. Even his spelling was incorrect."

Mitchell was a grand old man. His eyes would flash.
"In the matter of education and culture, we have shal-
low ideas. We forget that living experience of men and
things without which education is nothing. Washington and Lincoln were the luckiest of men. There is
no reason for fools to pity them. They were subjected
to one of the most powerful influences in the world,
the life of the frontier. To live with plain men in a

sparsely settled region gives one an insight into human character and the bases of human society nothing else equals. Washington was also lucky to be so often in the company of Lord Fairfax. Fairfax trained him by his companionship and affection, and he matured early. He was as much at home in the polite world as on the frontier, in regard not only to manners and clothes, but to what men and women talk about, and what they want life to be, for themselves and for others.

"A person who is our superior in knowledge, or moral character, or whatever, draws out of us latent powers, for we imitate what we admire. And what such people have to give us does not come coldly out of them as from books, but with the warmth of the sun. All education does not come from living people, but certainly all culture does."

What Langdon Mitchell had in mind was perhaps the problem of the opposites. Many city men try to solve it when it pinches them, by going hunting or fishing. And the procedure is correct, though the problem can be more serious. Kit Carson was no Lincoln and no Washington, but he had their American blood in his veins. So far as great human issues are concerned, he was in all his later life sound as an oak. The incentives to action which as a young man he naturally found outside himself, in middle age he began to find inside himself. Thus he solved the problem in its deepest form, and played the part of a man in the issues vital to human society.

He had to meet one of these issues in 1856 when Father Machebeuf went to Taos to pronounce the sentence of excommunication on Father Martinez, that able but rebellious priest who caused Bishop Lamy trouble. Martinez was suspected, unjustly I think, of having had more than a hand in the bloody uprising of a few years before, and people feared another such affair. Nothing happened over the excommunication, because Carson and a few other powerful residents were loyal to the Bishop and his aide. Carson expressed himself thus, "We will not let them du as they did in 1847, when they murdered and pillaged. I am a man of peace, and my motto is, good will to all. I hate disturbances among the people, but I can fight a little yit. I know of no better cause to fight for than my family, my church, and my friend Señor Vicario." It was largely a Mexican affair, since Martinez was greatly beloved by his countrymen. But Carson knew the nature of the conflicts inside the Mexican, for his wife was a native; and he chose the side of the quarrel to support which he felt to be more constructive for the future of both peoples.

Another example of his devotion to social purposes was his friendship for the Navajo. He had had more than a hunter's and fighter's knowledge of the Indian, for he had had two Indian wives, one an Arapaho

(who died) and one a Cheyenne (who deserted him
after some months of throwing dishpans at him). Spaniard, Mexican, U. S. American, had found the conquest
of the Navajo a long-drawn-out and bitter task. During the Civil War, when the garrisons were drained
of their soldiers, the Navajo and the Apache resumed
their former marauding. General J. H. Carleton, in
command of what troopers there were, decided on as
ruthless warfare as the Indians. His order in 1863
about the Mescalero Apaches is well known: "All Indian men of that tribe are to be killed whenever and
wherever you can find them." Kit Carson, now a
Colonel in the First Regiment of New Mexico Volunteers, was of course Carleton's right-hand man, for
no one ever surpassed him as an Indian fighter. Carleton overcame the Navajo in a number of fights, and
they retreated to their most inaccessible fastness, Canyon de Chelly. Here Carson was for once in command
of all the men he needed, and by shrewd tactics he
actually forced the tribe to surrender, taking seven
thousand prisoners.

Yet, when the Navajo were placed on a reservation
in a hot and fatal country, and kept there three desperate years, and were apparently to be kept there till
they died, he insisted that they be restored to their
native habitat, and it was done. He accomplished it
quietly, through his personal influence, and it is not
headlined on the pages of history. That the Navajo

live and multiply today is due largely to one man's sense of brotherliness and hatred of unnecessary suffering.

Lincoln had no Fairfax to befriend him, but he had a few great books. Carson had not even books. But what he did have, in his own modest fashion, was an ability like Lincoln's (and like Washington's) to absorb within him the best the frontier had to offer, and to see it as part of the best human life has to offer, and worth a hard fight to preserve.

Only one other scout in the history of the Southwest approaches the stature of Carson, and he was a different type of man. Jacob Hamblin lived to a good old age, and his monument at Alpine, Arizona, bears an inscription as interesting as that on Carson's obelisk at Santa Fe—"Peacemaker to the Camp of the Lamanites." The key to these mysterious words lies in the fact that the Mormons believe the Red Men to be the Lamanites of the Book of Mormon. Thus Hamblin was most careful in all his dealings with the Indian. He hoped he might bring him back to the right path if he were honest and patient enough. Because of his fair dealing the tribes held him in fully as high repute as Carson, and it can be said that his patience exceeded the latter's. The Mormon missionaries were much like the Spanish friars; they gave themselves with unwearied fervor to a cause that might well have brought martyrdom.

Hamblin first went into the Arizona country in 1857, and during succeeding years made repeated journeys under the direction of Brigham Young, president of the Mormons. It was Hamblin whom Young dispatched to the Hopi villages on the famous expedition to find out whether it was true that the Hopi language contained Welsh words. He had with him a Welsh miner named Durias Davis, who spoke Welsh, and a fifteen-year-old boy, Ammon M. Tenney, later a well-known scout, who knew Spanish and many Indian dialects. The three returned with a disappointing report, but one to be expected.

The following year Young sent Hamblin back to the Hopis with a missionary group to convert them. The Hopis were respectful and kind, but declined conversion. They said, "We can make no move until the three prophets come back who led our fathers and told them to stay on these rocks until they came again and told them what to do next."

In 1862 Hamblin led the first party of white men who ever circled the Grand Canyon. In 1870 he sat with Major J. W. Powell in a gathering of Shivwit Indians. They hoped to persuade the Indians to kill no more of Powell's highly trained geographers and ethnologists. Powell later said of Hamblin, "He is a silent, reserved man, and when he speaks it is in a slow, quiet way that inspires great awe. His talk is so low that the Indians must listen attentively to hear, and they sit around him in death-like silence."

Of the warm regard of the Indians for him his son, Jacob Hamblin, Junior, tells the following story:

"My father sent me to trade a horse with an old Navajo headman. I was just a boy, and rode my pony, leading the other horse. The old Indian came out and lifted me down.

"I said, 'Father wants to trade the horse for some blankets.'

"He brought out a number of handsome blankets, but father had said to be sure to make a good trade. So I shook my head and said such a valuable horse should bring still more. The old man then brought out two fine buffalo robes and more blankets, chief's blankets.

"When I got home with the roll, father went through them all, and put them in two piles. One pile was bigger than the other. It had the buffalo robes and the chief's blankets and certain other blankets. Father pointed to it and said, 'Take these back and tell the old man he sent me too many.'

"The old chief was waiting for me. He said, 'I knew you would come back. I knew Jacob would not keep so many; you know Jacob is *our* father as well as *your* father.'"

Hamblin's name is not commemorated in a place-

name in Arizona. The logical place would be Lee's
Ferry, below Cameron on the Colorado River, for he
repeatedly made that difficult crossing. When it might
be commemorating a man who tried all his life to
do what was right, it is odd for a commonwealth to
keep alive an unsavory name like Lee's. Lee was in
reality the notorious Major Doyle of the Mountain
Meadows massacre. (In defiance of Brigham Young,
some Mormons and many Paiutes combined to attack
a wagon train from Arkansas, reported to be coming
to attack the Mormons. The survivors, the children
especially, were badly treated, and Lee, or Doyle, was
accused of violating young girls. He hid out at the
ferry which bears his name, but returning to Utah for
provisions was captured, tried, and executed for his
crimes.) It would be confusing to change the name of
this ferry, which is not often mentioned, yet is kept
in mind retentively as a keypoint in giving directions
and routes. However, when the ferry became a bridge
not long ago it might have been done.

The country Hamblin was familiar with as a scout,
all that terrain of southern Utah and northern Arizona,
is as difficult as any in the world, and much of it is
still wild. Carson never encountered anything as bad.
The great chasm of the canyon in itself makes for
untold inconvenience. Fredonia, in Coconino County,
Arizona, is one hundred and forty-five miles by air
from the county seat, Flagstaff, but it is on the other

side of the canyon, and until quite recently the easiest way of communication was via Utah and Nevada, a distance of a thousand miles. In this limited yet man-defeating area Hamblin performed giant-like tasks, but they were humble and those of the missionary, the pathfinder, the emissary. Thus it happens that only the people of northern Arizona and the Mormon historians are in a position to appreciate his services and his character. Carson held the great stage of the world, Hamblin an out-of-the-way and little-known stage, but they were both good men and they were equals, for they were honest.

17. The Mormon Battalion

The new marker to commemorate the Mormon Battalion will be seen on the highway about fifteen miles north of Algodones. . . .
        —Albuquerque, New Mexico, Tribune

ONLY a year or so after the occupation of Santa Fe by federal troops, the Mormon Battalion had marched across the whole of the Southwest to California.

By 1846 the Mormons had come to the conclusion that the people of Illinois would never let them live in peace and they had better move on. The church sent its president, Jesse C. Little, to Washington to confer with President Polk about federal assistance in the trek westward. The Mormons thought Polk might employ them to build stockades along an overland route. They were considering making California their goal. The chief result of the conference was that the church accepted Polk's proposal to enlist a Mormon military command for dispatch to the Pacific coast.

Thus the Mormon Battalion was part of the volunteer soldiery of the Mexican war. The regular army was small; General Winfield Scott was holding it for descent on Vera Cruz. The northern army in Mexico was largely volunteer. Colonel Alexander W. Doniphan marched to Chihuahua with volunteers from Missouri. California could not have been seized from Mexico unless General S. W. Kearny's small force of dragoons had been reinforced.

Captain James Allen of the First Dragoon regiment, who recruited the battalion, said in his circular, "This gives an opportunity of sending a portion of your young and intelligent men to the ultimate destination of your whole people at the expense of the United States, and this advance party can pave the way and look out the land for their brethren."

The recruiting officer was greatly surprised that every man could write his own name. Only one in three of the Missouri volunteers had been so accomplished. Five companies were mustered in and given antiquated equipment, flintlock muskets, with a few caplocks for hunting. They left Fort Leavenworth July 20, 1846, and reached Santa Fe along the old trail, October 9. Doniphan, who was in command of the post, welcomed them warmly with a salute of one hundred guns. He was an old friend of the Mormons, for as a lawyer in Clay County, Missouri, he had succeeded in changing a judgment of death passed by the mob on Joseph Smith.

Captain Allen died en route, and Captain Philip

St. George Cooke, of the dragoons, took over the battalion. We have his description of it. "It was enlisted too much by families; some were too old, some feeble, and some too young; it was embarrassed by too many women; it was undisciplined; it was too much worn by travel on foot; clothing was very scant; there was no money to pay them or clothing to issue; their mules were utterly broken down; animals scarce and inferior and deteriorating every hour for lack of forage." Allen sent the families to Pueblo and reshaped the companies to 448 men. Against everybody's advice, but correctly, he insisted that the wagons be taken along no matter in what shape the mules were.

The battalion left Santa Fe, October 19, crossed the summit of the Rockies, November 28, captured Tucson from the Mexicans, December 18, reached the mouth of the Gila, January 8, and arrived near San Diego on January 29. It was the first march overland, the first passage of wagons across the deserts and mountains, and it would be difficult to find its duplicate for speed and for endurance. Captain Cooke, now a Lieutenant Colonel, found it well to be democratic with his men, for he discovered that they talked back. One Mormon youth told him to go to hell when he kept ordering him to ford a swollen river. Considering that Cooke was a West Pointer, the way he adapted himself to his not at all warlike, really farmer-like, command, and led them safely to their goal, sharing

thirst, starvation, and sun blisters with them, is an exploit of its own. He came to admire his men intensely,
and at San Diego issued a remarkable order in their
praise:

"The Lieutenant Colonel congratulates the battalion
on their march of over two thousand miles.

"History may be searched in vain for an equal march
of infantry. Half of it has been through a wilderness,
where nothing but savages and wild beasts are found,
or deserts where there is no living creature. There,
with almost hopeless labor, we have dug wells which
the future traveler will enjoy.

"Without a guide we have ventured into trackless
tablelands; with crowbar and pick, and ax in hand,
we have worked our way over mountains and hewed
a pass for our wagons. . . . We have preserved the
strength of our mules by herding them over large
tracts. . . .

"Thus, marching half naked and half fed, and living upon wild animals, we have made a road of great
value to our country. . . .

"Arrived at the first settlements of California, after
a single day's rest, volunteers, you have cheerfully
turned off from the route to meet the approach of an
enemy; and this too without even salt to season your
sole subsistence of fresh meat."

Only at the conclusion of his order does Lieutenant
Colonel Cooke remind us that he is a West Pointer.

It is sad, yet he does wind up by saying, "But much remains undone. Soon you will turn your attention to the drill, to system and order. . . ."

A year later gold was discovered at Sutter's Creek. But Brigham Young and his pioneers had reached the Salt Lake Valley six months before. The church distrusted the effect of easy wealth on human nature, and on their discharge called back the battalion members to earn their living on the land and by the sweat of their brow. Practically all of them obeyed the summons, and a good many battalion members became the pioneer settlers of Arizona. Their photographs in old age impress one; they have grand faces and grand beards. They seem like a race apart.

18. Snowflake

Snowflake will hold its annual rodeo as usual on July 24. . . .

—*Prescott*, Arizona, *Evening Courier*

THERE are many Mormon settlements in northern Arizona and a few in New Mexico, like Aztec. Snowflake was founded in July, 1878. James Stinson, a non-Mormon, was the pioneer in this valley, which lies twenty-eight miles south of Holbrook. Settled there five years, he had taken out the waters of Silver Creek for the irrigation of some 300 acres. When the first Mormons came along, Stinson sold to their representative, William J. Flake, for $11,000 paid in livestock. Two months later Erastus Snow, in charge of pioneer Arizona colonization for the Mormon church, visited the scene and found it "a nice little valley." Flake's ranch was everyone's choice as a townsite, and Snow and Flake joined surnames to give the place a name. Soon after New Year's Day, a group of families who had failed to find land at St. Johns joined those at Snowflake. Thus augmented, the colony prepared to divide the property. It was surveyed with ditch lines, and the settlers drew by lot for the farming land in two parcels of ten acres each. Each settler had these twenty acres and also a city plot, the whole valued at $200 or ten head of stock. It was at the rate Flake had paid for the entire property.

Like all Mormon towns, Snowflake is laid out with an eye to the future. You can tell a Mormon town anywhere. The streets are broad and the houses have ample space about them, and the trees are tall and handsome. Other Mormon towns are near Snowflake, some like St. Joseph and Taylor antedating it, others coming later, like Shumway (named after a Patriarch of the Church) and Showlow. The latter is a pre-Mormon name, deriving from a game of seven-up in which the players wagered their various possessions. One Clark at last exclaimed, "Show low and you take the ranch." One Cooley showed low and took it.

The Mormons had first attempted to settle northern Arizona five years before the Snowflake stake, in 1873. The first group to cross the Colorado crossed it at Lee's Ferry; from Utah, northern Arizona is extremely difficult of access. Nothing came of this expedition; there were too many Apaches, too much alkali, and too little water. Henry Holmes kept a journal. He remarks that the land "was barren and forbidding, although doubtless the Lord had a purpose in view when he made it so." Holmes was astonished to find petrified logs in this treeless land. One of them was 210 feet long. Another was six feet across the butt. He observes, "I do not know that it makes any difference whether the country is barren or fruitful, if the Lord has a work to do in it." This characteristic remark refers to more than missionary effort, for reclaiming land was to the pioneer Mormon as good as reclaiming Indians, or almost as good.

When three years later, settlers began digging in at Sunset Crossing and St. Joseph, they found the Little Colorado hard to harness. Their first dam cost $5,000 and 960 days of work, their first ditch 500 days' more work. Both dam and ditch went in the first flood. Dam followed dam, and in 1894 Andrew Jenson said the community had lost $50,000 on its dams. He called St. Joseph "the leading community in pain, determination and unflinching courage in dealing with the elements around them."

Possibly no church organization ever put more strength behind its pioneers than did the Mormon. The church never let any of them down, and the settlements never let one another down. This inter-webbing of mutual aid is a force we know too little about. It makes oases in the desert. I like to think of it that way; then it seems something we can grasp.

Leonora Curtin, who is a great traveler, in fact a world traveler, happened in at Snowflake one mid-afternoon in July, and liked the look of the quiet shady town, the green fields, and the gleaming reservoir. She was en route from Keam's Canyon on an archaeological trip, and had met three Mormons on the road, big blond Viking men as so many of them are. They directed her to Auntie Pearl's (all elderly Mormon women are called Auntie). Not finding Auntie Pearl at first she investigated a neat sign at the barber's, "Bath, 25 cents." The barber (a non-Mormon) mistook her for an itinerant optician. Later she inquired about it of her oculist in Albuquerque, and learned that in spite of efforts of the profession to license their traveling brethren, one such optician was still at large somewhere in the vicinity of Holbrook.

While Leonora Curtin and the barber were threshing out the question of her identity, he and his wife showed her round their place, with its well-taken-care-of apple trees dating from the early days of the town. She asked where she might get supper, and he indicated a Greek restaurant on the main street. But she remembered Auntie Pearl, and he took her to a neat red-brick house with a white porch and a yard full of flowers. On the way she learned that the Greek restaurateur was a newcomer, who had been able to gain his foothold in the face of opposition by the elders of the church. He ran a pool hall and a bar, also. Many young men went there evenings, and spent at least ten cents a night, money they could ill afford. Money is scarce in these Mormon towns, for nearly all transactions are by barter. Some towns have had successful co-operative stores, and Snowflake once had such a store, but it was no longer in existence. Leonora Curtin told me of sitting on the step of such a store at Monticello, when a little girl came out with an all-day sucker. "How did you get that?" she inquired. "I thwapped an egg for it," said the child. In the eighties the co-operative movement among the Mormons roused great interest; Edward Bellamy wrote *Looking Backward* after a long interview with Erastus Snow, president of the church, in 1886, regarding the operation of the United Order Plan.

A bar in a Mormon town is a discordant note, for the church forbids the faithful even tea and coffee; in addition, Snowflake and several near-by towns have a gentlemen's agreement not to sell tobacco.

Auntie Pearl had just come home from helping a sixteen-year-old girl, whose mother had died, put up a hundred quarts of fruit that day. She was a generous provider. Leonora Curtin told us that supper consisted of home-canned "beef" (really venison and known as long-legged Mormon mutton), mashed potatoes, corn, beets, hot biscuit, tomatoes, and peaches, milk, honey, jelly, hot apple pie, all of it delicious. Auntie Pearl asked whether fifty cents would be satisfactory. Seventy-five cents would be better, said Leonora.

"Oh, my, I was never paid so much for a meal in all my life," said Auntie Pearl.

The breakfast next morning was waffles, honey, coffee, cream too thick to pour, and fruit. The coffee was bad; but Auntie Pearl admitted that her husband had always made his coffee himself. She lives on half an acre, and being a widow pays no taxes. Her water and light cost her five dollars a month. She grows and cans enough vegetables for her family. She has four daughters and a son at home, two daughters working in Holbrook, and a married son; and she has seven grandchildren.

For their amusement, the eight or nine hundred citizens of Snowflake can go to the movie twice a month, and after the movie to a dance. The rodeo comes once a year, the tickets for the show, including barbecue, beans, meat, and pickles, with dessert extra, being one dollar. Every house has a barbecue in the front yard, for the church fosters social gatherings, and Mormons have good appetites. Snowflake possesses a handsome temple, but Leonora did not have time to visit it, if indeed visits are permitted. Snowflake has also an Academy, built in 1921 at a cost of $35,000 to replace a previous academy which had burnt down. The Mormons believe in schooling.

Mrs. Wall, the barber's wife, told Leonora that she loved the townspeople and would live nowhere else, everyone was "so kind and sweet." It is the sort of comment one hears about Mormons and Mormon towns. They are the shyest of the various kinds and sorts of people who live in the piñon country, and you rarely see the word Mormon in a newspaper. Their religion gives them a deep interest in land, a real bond with it; except for the Pueblo Indians, nobody has done so much to make the desert blossom.

What interests me out of the ordinary is that the Mormons in the course of making northern Arizona blossom (in places) lost only thirty-one of their members from violent deaths of the kind associated with frontier life. The church keeps detailed records of its history, and the late James H. McClintock, State Historian of Arizona, studied them in connection with his own files and considered the number an accurate accounting. Three of these deaths were caused by accidents, such as drowning in the Colorado River, and may well be omitted from the total. Of the remaining twenty-eight, eight were officers of the law slain in the line of duty by white fugitives from justice, so that it is hardly in point to count them, either; the murder of law-enforcement officers goes on endlessly. Of the other deaths, thirst took three, Mexicans two, Paiutes four, the Navajo five, and Apaches seven. Settling along the Colorado and in the vicinity of the Grand Canyon, the Mormons were in the haunts of particularly fierce Indian nations, so that the wonder of it grows. One group of white people moved into the

Southwest without driving the Indians frantic, slaughtering and being slaughtered by them. The Mormons did not come heavily armed. They were thinking about the land itself and about being friends with the Indians, not about gold mines or dispossessing anybody.

A story like that of the Greek who forced his way into Snowflake with pool hall and bar makes you wonder whether the young Mormons of today are growing up without losing continuity with their past. The only Mormons I see are young men who come to my house once a year, generally in late summer, in the missionary cause. They have told me it is a requirement of their college education to go out into the world and spread the gospel, and they seem secure in the belief that their gospel is *the* gospel. At present the Mormons number about one-twelfth of the population of Arizona, and it may be the stablest and most important twelfth. They have given names to more than a hundred and fifty places in the state. But there is little land or water left to divide, and the days of pioneering are now over. Certainly the elder Mormons found a means of living with themselves and with others. It came from a certain right focussing of attention, and I hope their children are making the transition from early conditions to conditions of today without losing that secret focus.

Working with earth and water is different from working with machines. While you can add a machine to a man safely, it seems difficult to add a man to a machine without tearing his life out of him. The new pioneering is the will to add machines to men, not men to machines. Husbanding the penurious land and at peace with themselves, the Mormons contributed infinitesimal oases of shade and moisture to the vast parched country where they came to live. They did not add themselves to the desert so much as the desert to themselves, and so where they touched it they changed it. And that is why all who touch their fringes seem to find peace, too, if only momentarily. This drawing of land, or machines, or anything else, into the human measure is no philosophy of contraction, no fear or shrinking up from existence, but a shepherding by people of one another, a plowing and watering of the humanity held in common, above all an attitude towards life of vigilant welcome.

19. The Pioneer Presses

This year marks the seventy-fifth anniversary of the founding of the *Arizona Miner*—on Granite Creek—where the city of Prescott now stands. At that time Tucson was the only other American settlement in what is now Arizona. . . .

—*Prescott*, Arizona, *Evening Courier*, 1939

PRESIDENT LINCOLN appointed territorial officials to Arizona in 1863. On their way west they purchased a printing press in Santa Fe, and took it along, though they did not know where they were going. Tucson was the only point at which there were traces of an American settlement, but Tucson was unsavory because of its Confederate record. The party established itself on Granite Creek, now the site of Prescott. The Apache felt quite at his ease in this region, and when the *Arizona Miner* appeared the following year the printing of it, like the plowing for the settlement, had to be done under military protection. The typesetter, like the plowman, had his rifle under his arm. Yet in its second year the paper's editor, a twenty-seven-year-old youth named Bentley, was slain by Apaches in his very office. The paper continued as

Marion's Miner, passing into the hands of an editor
who vigorously denounced "eastern philanthropists"
and the Indian policy of the government. At one time
it reached seven hundred subscribers. Marion later
said he spent ten years editing the sheet, all the while
"a little alarmed about the permanency of our scalp."

The *Arizona Miner* was not, however, the first newspaper in Arizona. In a museum at Tucson, passing a
quiet old age, is a Washington hand-press, with lever.
When it was young this press took a trip round the
Horn from Baltimore to the Port of Guaymas and
thence was hauled north by tedious oxcart. In 1859 it
found itself in Tubac, a settlement of four hundred
Mexican and Papago souls, with a sprinkling of Americans. That year the Salaro Mining Company, its pro-
prietors, founded a newspaper, *The Weekly Arizonian,*
with Edward Cross as editor. The early issues adver-
tise the whiskey you could buy in Tubac, and other
things you could send to Cincinnati for. The news
deals with prospecting parties, horse-stealing, and
Apache atrocities: Two prospectors die of eating a
plant called wild parsnip. A soldier who deserted from
Fort Buchanan to turn horse-thief is sentenced to receive fifty lashes with a cowhide and to be branded
with the letter D.

Arizona at this time was still part of New Mexico,
but there was already agitation for its recognition as
a separate territory. The leader in the movement was

a twenty-six-year-old Lieutenant Mowry, sent out from West Point when Fort Yuma was being built. Mowry surrendered his imagination to the Arizona landscape. Maps of the country were his meditation day and night. Remarkably enough, he could vision the region even then as a political entity with a human future of its own, not merely as a land where mining companies might grow rich and then depart, leaving it more arid even than they found it. Mowry's enthusiasm led him into conflict with Editor Cross of *The Weekly Arizonian*. Cross, a veteran of the Mexican war, was opposed to territorial recognition. He called the idea "preposterous, premature and not feasible." Mowry he charged with fabricating population figures to impress the federal government, and from figures he went on to assail Mowry's personal reputation. The result was a duel with Burnside rifles at forty paces. Mowry's rifle failed to discharge at the last exchange. The seconds decided he was entitled to another shot, and Cross stood with arms folded to receive it. Mowry shot into the air and declared himself satisfied. San Francisco and New York papers retailed the incident to urban readers with embellishments, such as that a seventy-mile gale was blowing across the line of fire.

Mowry bought the paper, and took it to Tucson. He continued to publish it until the Civil War. Tucson people were predominantly southern in their sympathies, and Mowry was no exception. The town hoisted the Confederate flag. But in 1862 the California Column, federal troops hastily assembled on the West coast, captured Tucson for the Union. Mowry was imprisoned on charges of conspiracy, and his mines, then yielding $700 a day, were confiscated. Later they were restored for lack of proof. This man of extraordinary vision died while still young, in a London hotel.

The first library in Arizona was a collection of books Samuel Colt, inventor of the Colt revolver, dispatched from the West coast to his Cerro Colorado mine at Arivaca, for the miners to read. A trooper in a small detachment of the California Column stationed at the mine came across Prescott's three-volume story of the Mexican conquest, and was amazed that print could mean such color, action, and entertainment. His name was Edward E. Ayer; he was twenty-two years old, and Prescott's was the first book he ever finished. He finished it three times, and it was to influence his life greatly. When he died many years later, he left the Newberry Library of Chicago (one of the most pleasant libraries in the world to browse about in) a collection of Americana worth several million dollars.

Today the life of a newspaper is as much in its advertising as in its editorial columns. Such a view of journalism the pioneers would have thought poltroonery. Nor had they any idea of the funnies and other departments by which the contemporary paper endears itself. As for advertising there was only one paper in the early Southwest that ever carried much of it, a Spanish paper, founded in Tucson in 1878, *Las Dos Republicas*. It attracted eastern attention because it circulated in Sonora, Chihuahua, and Sinaloa, and had more readers than one would expect. Editorially it warned Mexicans not to become citizens of the States, under threat of ridicule—a threat which it would carry out.

Through all the southwestern states from Louisiana to Arizona the early printing presses were candles trying hard to stay lighted in the dark winds of violence.

The first printing job in the whole region came from the press of Denis Braud of New Orleans, *Imprimeur du Roi,* in 1764. It was the tardy announcement of Louis XV that two years before, he had handed Louisiana over to Spain by a secret treaty. A true member of the ruling class, Louis XV saw land only in terms of barter and diplomacy; the people on the land went with it the way trees and rivers do. Later Denis Braud printed a petition to His Majesty to take the province back again. For the first Spanish governor proved so unpopular that the council of citizens asked him to get out, and he did so. Then Spain sent an Irishman, Alexander O'Reilly, with 3,000 soldiers to discipline Louisiana. O'Reilly executed six of the leading citizens, and among those he imprisoned was Denis Braud. Braud was later released on his plea that as official printer he had no other alternative than to publish the treason-able pamphlet. The treason of it was that the people dared tell the king they were not trees and rivers, and had a right to be heard regarding the ownership of the land they lived on. Louis XV gives Louisiana to Spain without a qualm. Lieutenant Mowry anxiously visions a future Arizona for people to live in rather than for mining companies to squeeze dry. The difference between the two attitudes is still the foremost problem of the Southwest.

In Texas the first printer of record was one Samuel Bangs, who sailed from Baltimore for Galveston with a revolutionary expedition. In 1817 he printed the proclamation of the General against existing Mexican rule. Bangs was captured by the government forces, and imprisoned at Saltillo, the capital at that time of Texas and Coahuila. A copy of a periodical printed at Nacogdoches in 1813, four years before Bangs's *Proclama,* still exists, but nothing is known of it nor its editor. It was a candle snuffed out as soon as lighted. In 1819, also at Nacogdoches, two Americans issued a sheet called the *Texas Republican.* It shed its light for two months. Then the government of Mexico captured the town and destroyed the printing office and equipment. For the next few years American newspapers came thick and fast, all of them short-lived. They were issued at Brazoria, San Felipe de Austin, Monterey, Matamoros, and San Antonio. Most of their editors survived in one shape or another. It is worthy of note that wherever they go, Americans promptly start newspapers. Other races wait until the time is ripe, but to the American a medium of expression is always in order, and for it he will give his life, if he has to. The instinct at work here may or may not be the same that produced the Town Meeting; I rather think it is.

In New Mexico, so far as I can make out, the first press was one purchased in Chihuahua by Don Santiago Abreu in 1833 when he passed through that town en route to Mexico City as a delegate to the Mexican assembly. It reached Santa Fe by oxcart the following year, a distance of 600 miles. Don Ramón, brother to Don Santiago, tried to operate it, but luckily for him a printer soon came up from Durango. This printer, named Baca, was to follow the press from one owner to another for many years, the sole printer for a thousand miles. His first job was the notice to the Town Council of Santa Fe that Don Ramón Abreu was embarking in the newspaper business with a journal called *The Dawn of Liberty,* published in the interests of Don Antonio Barreiro, candidate for re-election as deputy to the Mexican assembly.

Barreiro and the brothers Abreu were forward-looking men. Don Antonio had already submitted to the authorities in Mexico a survey of conditions in the northern colony. He says, "Liberty of the Press, this inestimable good, is the same as dead for the Territory because no press exists, nor do newspapers circulate to spread abroad that public spirit which is the soul of republican liberty. . . . Another obstacle to enlightenment no less is the enormous distance at which this place lies, and our lack of communication with the interior of the Republic."

The men responsible for these early presses were extraordinary creatures. It is a pity we know so little about them. The fascinating and enigmatic Padre Martinez was at this time flourishing in Taos, he who said a republic was a better burro for lawyers than for priests. He opened a school at Taos the same year that saw the founding of *The Dawn of Liberty* in Santa Fe. Though the Abreus still owned it, he apparently took over this newspaper. But there were too few people who could read to keep a paper going, and the padre discontinued it after the fourth issue. To insure a more robust future for newspapers he proceeded humbly and wisely to the indicated task of teaching people their ABC's. Thus it came about that the first book published in New Mexico was a speller.

Padre Martinez's speller appeared a year or so before the first book published in Texas after it became a republic. This was a historical document, the *Evacuation of Texas*, translated from General Filisola's representation to his government in defense of his honor, a volume not without balm for Texans.

The first book published in New Orleans antedated

these two volumes by some sixty years. It was a legal work, the famous Code Noir, for the administration of justice, discipline, and sale of slaves. The cultural difference between the east coast and the states of the interior is shown further, for within a few months of the Code Noir, Antoine Boudousquié, the official printer, also brought out a pamphlet, *La Prise du Morne du Baton Rouge,* which actually contained verse, a *Poème* and a *Chanson* by one Julien Poydras.

Arizona's first book appeared in 1860, *Constitution and Schedule of the Provisional Government of the Territory of Arizona, and the Proceedings of the Convention held at Tucson.* That this should be Arizona's first volume will surprise no one who knows the history of the state and its brave political self-consciousness.

The first book published in what is now Oklahoma comes surprisingly early, 1835, but its nature will be no surprise if you know your Oklahoma. It was *The Child's Book,* printed in the Creek language, a twenty-four-page illustrated pamphlet run off a press at Union Mission. Rev. Samuel A. Worcester, an American Board Missionary from New England, had brought this press with him from Georgia where he first used it among the Cherokees. Worcester also issued almanacs for 1836 in the Cherokee and Choctaw languages. The first presses of Indian Territory could hardly be called candles in a gale. They were noticed far and wide; a Paris newspaper, even, hailed and blessed them. Circumstances were in their favor; the *Cherokee Advocate,* for instance, founded in 1844, continued with a few interruptions until 1907. Other striking examples of continuity in the southwest region are the present *Times-Picayune* of New Orleans, with a record of continuous publication from 1842 to the present, except for two months during the reconstruction period, and the *Santa Fe New Mexican,* with a record, also with interruptions, of publication from 1849. Both these newspapers have survived many a hurricane.

Early presses represent what is going on in their regions and Padre Martinez's spelling book was among the few and last evidences of the northern Spaniards' desire to improve conditions. The total of such evidence for the two centuries of Spanish rule is not impressive. Unfortunately, in the uprising of 1837 the brothers Santiago and Ramón Abreu were tortured and killed. Their printing press comes into sight again five years later, in the possession of Donaciano Vigil. Vigil used it to publish a newspaper called *La Verdad* (The Truth), issued at Santa Fe on Thursdays. An extant issue describes depredations by Ute Indians near Chimayo. *The Truth* did not last more than two years; the uprising in Mexico against Santa Ana apparently ended it. The press then passed into the hands of Governor José

Chavez, who put out a newspaper called *The Country-man*, and incidentally paid for it at state expense. The prospectus of this paper says of its predecessor, "*The Truth* died at the beginning of May as the result of an acute disorder it contracted from the strong wind that blew from the south of Mexico on the twentieth of November." But the acute disorder that killed it was really the surrounding illiteracy, which had already killed Padre Martinez's paper, and was soon to kill *The Countryman* itself. Articles in the two issues preserved in the Bancroft Library include a letter from the Archbishop of Durango instructing New Mexico churches to pray for the deliverance of Mexico City from earthquakes. A political article states that Santa Ana had based his government on vice, prostitution, and brigandage. The only article apropos to conditions in New Mexico would seem still to be apropos. It complains of government waste in maintaining needless offices and employees, while workers and farmers have to sell their tools to pay the oppressive taxes.

There is reason for tracing to the bitter end the history of this Chihuahua printing press. After the United States Americans moved in, it promptly came to life again. Hovey and Davies bought it in 1847 to issue a four-page newspaper, *The Santa Fe Republican*. The reader is advised that the columns will be devoted to "science, agriculture, the earliest news from the United States and the general movement of the army." The paper also boasted a motto, "We die but never surrender," for the Southwest breeds rhetorical flourishes. Whether the editors died or surrendered, the paper did not last long, ceasing to follow the movement of the army the following year. We then lose sight of our printing press until 1869, when the Maxwell Land Grant Cattle Company at Cimarron was using it to print *The Cimarron News and Press.* On Saturday nights the cowboys from Elizabethtown, Cimarron, and Red River were accustomed to do as they pleased in Cimarron. They made people dance by shooting at their feet, and invented practical jokes perhaps amusing, certainly objectionable. After one bad time of this sort, their employers took them to task for their conduct in an editorial in the company paper. The following Saturday night the cowboys, who could dish out trouble to others but could not take even a rebuke themselves, broke into the office of the *News,* chopped up the press, and threw the pieces into the Cimarron River. The drunken deed ended a press that had never known anything approaching peace, but only civil strife, international strife, and the endless strife against ignorance.

Now we find ourselves in a very different world from that of pioneer days. The Southwest has become part of the world of communication. The church already in residence has profited greatly by its release from former isolation. Other churches have moved in, some of them with high ideals of social responsibility. The public school has moved in, and so has the public library. And so have the state universities, and following the example of Harvard they have within ten years begun to establish presses. The great problems of the region, in respect to poverty, health, illiteracy, and erosion and weather, and business, politics, and culture, have in no way lessened but steadily increased. But now the social forces to attack them are gathering, and are growing stronger for the formidable adventure.

It all amounts to a significant though provincial episode in the long history of printing. Just as nearly all the Southwest is cut off from the rest of the country and given different weather conditions by not being in the path of the cyclonic storms that come roaring from the Mackenzie basin to New England—so also is it different by reason of close contact with the ways of other races, the Negro, the Navajo, and the Pueblo Indians, the Spaniard, and the Frenchman, and also with the southern or cavalier tradition of our own race, with a minimum of the industrial and non-agrarian tradition of the East. It will be a great strength to us in our region if we can feel these psychic forces and know that they too are rightful features of human life, contributing to the praise, the beauty and the worship of the marvelous world.

20. The Kid

A new gravestone for souvenir hunters to chisel, and a seven-foot spiked-top fence to keep them from doing it, Thursday marked the resting place of Billy the Kid, youthful desperado of early territorial days.

The new marker, made of Colorado granite, was donated by James N. Warner, Salida, Colo., monument maker, who carved into it all the data he could gather.

The 75-year-old graveyard, abandoned to weeds and pumpkin vines, is crowded between farmers' fields five miles southeast of here. It holds the bodies of more than a hundred, including the great landowner, Lucien Maxwell, and his wife, Luz, famous beauty of the Beaubien family, and also Juanita Garrett, first wife of the Sheriff Pat Garrett whose gun ended the bloody career of the Kid.

—*Fort Sumner*, New Mexico, *Leader*

THE PREVIOUS gravestone cost two hundred and eighty dollars, and was the gift of the residents of Fort Sumner. It was taken away bit by bit by souvenir hunters.

The growth of the Kid's fame is remarkable. As a source of revenue he begins to rival the Grand Canyon or the Carlsbad Caverns. So, in a region that draws all possible profit from travelers, it is not considered too shameful to capitalize on a morbid interest, and make a state monument of a museum devoted to a young wretch.

The Kid does not exhaust the interest of the Lincoln County war, however. It takes only a moment to get the high points of his career. Something the state might well do, which would interest most tourists, would be to give away at the various shrines to the Kid leaflets about the human implications of the story. One of these leaflets might be a psychologist's contrast between the Kid and his employer, Tunstall. Tunstall was an Englishman with a handsome dreamy face, the face of an idealist. He disbelieved that men could be as dangerous as he was warned the Lincoln County men were. He disbelieved he would be shot. Even when he saw Murphy's men riding towards him and his men, and greatly outnumbering them, he refused his foreman's advice to ride back with the others to the ranch house, where they could fight off attack. He was soon lying dead in the road. Tunstall with his English education and background could not adapt himself to Lincoln County, and it is a wonder he lived in Lincoln as long as a year and a half. The Kid was born in Brooklyn, but had spent part of his boyhood in Texas and is supposed to have killed his first man at the age of twelve. He seemed to fit in well in a region where men were far more dangerous than rattlers, but his nature was not formed, and it grew in accordance with his surroundings. If he had stayed in Brooklyn he might have become a choir-singer. Mrs. Ealy, in Lincoln at the time of the battle, says he often came to practice singing with other cowboys. "He seemed especially fond of music. He showed also a knowledge of the Christian hymns and sang them beautifully. He told me he attended Sunday school when at home."

In the five months the Ealys lived in Lincoln, Dr. Ealy preached funeral sermons for thirty persons, and only one of them had died a natural death. But if the Kid was shaped by his surroundings, he was also doomed by them. If you kill a man you start something out of your power to stop. His friends will not rest easy till they kill you. And if you elude them and keep on killing, you give your neighborhood a bad name, and law-abiding people won't come and live there. You are bad for business, because business depends on the law-abiding, and that finishes you. The posses will hunt you down like a coyote.

A leaflet explaining such matters ought to interest people, especially young persons cherishing the dream of great badness. There might even be a leaflet explaining the perennial nature of lawlessness. Driven from their spectacular roles, the bad men do not vanish from the sight of God. They bob up in a new place, namely politics. Politics offers them a chance to persist, with its plunder and its factional warfare, generally but not always bloodless. Only when they go too far and become bad for business by driving away law-abiding people, are they cleaned out of politics. It does not seem to me too much to suggest that a commonwealth might disseminate such knowledge.

There might be another leaflet too discussing the anomalous conduct of Colonel N. A. Dudley at Fort Stanton during the Lincoln County battle. A year later, when Governor Lew Wallace had Dudley removed because of his partisanship, the editor of the *Mesilla Independent*, a brave country newspaperman who should be remembered, wrote, "Had it been a year earlier, it might have saved a number of lives. Certainly McSween and his companions would not have been butchered as they were had it not been for the presence of Col. Dudley and troops under his command, and the aid he openly gave the other party [Murphy and Dolan]. This act alone did more to cripple and deaden the efforts of the orderly citizens of the county and to alarm and deter peaceably disposed people, than any act ever committed in the county by outlaws."

As the Kid was an employee of McSween and Tunstall, this comment shows how the supposed forces of law and order can be responsible for driving a boy into desperate ways. The comment is not to be dismissed as idle by current partisans in the matter (for the Lincoln County war is far from over in the books). Judge Frank W. Angel of New York City investigated Lin-

coln County for the government in the summer of
1878. He summarized the situation thus, "Both fac-
tions have done many things contrary to law. McSween
I firmly believe acted conscientiously; Murphy and Co.
for private gain and revenge."

Personally I possess the psychology of the tourist,
for I find the Kid interesting. But I find the whole story
worth while—every bit as worth while as any little journey to the home of a celebrated author. It uncovers
the base of society, and what makes communities stable and good and what does not. And the tourist would
find the whole story interesting, too, if the Tourist Bureau supplied him with leaflets about the ring of army
and Indian supply contractors who infested the country at the time, with whom Murphy and Dolan were
affiliates in fraudulent practices toward the government; and about the psychology of the chief persons
involved, and the psychology of business, and of
growth and progress. Mrs. Ealy's account of her Lincoln County days, as edited by Major Fulton, a manu-
script I had the pleasure of publishing in the *New
Mexico Sentinel*, would be an eye-opening leaflet in
itself.

As time goes on and competition increases, it may
be found well to deal with the understanding of tourists as well as their desires in the matter of highways,
cafés, and cabins.

Frances Otis of Santa Fe once met a CCC boy in the Monument Valley country, and gave him a ride. He was from Pittsburgh, and told her he had stood up in the vestibule of the coach all the way west so as not to miss any of the country. He was so excited by Arizona he hoped never to leave it.

Every visitor, every tourist zooming through this landscape will take away a few images, I don't care how fast he goes. Violet mountains gliding along the horizon like a fleet of battleships. The glowing embers of the stars in a tremendous stretch of night. Stars like Roman candles arrested and frozen in their bursting. Great dark clouds, splashes of milk-white luminousness, walking rain, red rain walking, shafts of intense sun through the blockades of vapor on the mountains. A Navajo riding his pony by a red butte. A dust-storm swirling up a dry river-bed and starting overland. An abandoned farm where a dry farmer lost his fight with the country. A coyote tied to a tree near a filling station. A rattlesnake or Gila monster in a box by a wayside museum where they sell petrified wood and Indian pottery. The white cyclamen of daybreak past a peak two hundred miles away.

Something will stick to even the swiftest, the sleepiest, the most indifferent. Gossamers of images will cling to eyelids and eyelashes. Gossamers of thought will cling to fringes of the mind, from the ever-shifting mirage of color and form on the long straight black roads. And so in Arizona and New Mexico the bureaus in charge of tourists bear a complex but engrossing task. What people go away thinking is more important than what their eyes remember.

21. The Bandits

Henry Lorenz, 22, and Harry Dwyer, 27, were given 50-75 years by District Judge Numa Frenger Saturday on their pleas of guilty to second degree murder. . . .

—*Las Cruces,* New Mexico, *Sun-News*

IT IS the old story of two eastern boys who wanted to play Billy the Kid. Southern Pacific train No. 11, known as "The Apache," westbound, left El Paso at 11:54 P.M. November 24, 1937, and a few moments later at Mt. Riley in Doña Ana County, New Mexico, near Las Cruces, it was held up by two young men who had been riding in the daycoach. One of them marched the conductor up the aisle, collecting money and jewelry from passengers on the right, while his confederate followed, robbing those on the left. They got very little, a few one-dollar bills, a twenty-dollar bill, some rings and watches. A little nurse protested that she needed her watch, and they gave it back to her. The two young robbers did not keep together. The one who was ahead ordered the conductor to stop the train, and he was about to get off when he heard a commotion behind him. His pal had been tripped and was lying in the aisle, with angry passengers pinning him down. Others were rising from their seats, among them a man who stood head and shoulders above the rest. The robber at the end of the car lifted his gun and shot and killed the tall man. He was an employee of the railroad, named W. L. Smith, thirty-five years old, and was en route from El Paso to San Francisco. The robber fired again and hit another passenger, also an employee of the railroad. But the bullet struck a metal cigarette case in the man's pocket, and he found it later in the cuff of his trousers.

Thanksgiving evening a posse brought the two young men to the county jail at Las Cruces. The one who had been tripped had his eye nearly knocked from its socket, the other was livid with bruises. Both were battered and miserable. In jail they were held incommunicado for several days, and thus in all probability never laid eyes on the big black headlines of the newspapers, nor heard the radio accounts of the hold-up. They came to trial February 19, 1938, in District Court, Las Cruces. On advice of their attorney, T. Benson Newell, who was appointed by the court to defend them, they made their plea of guilty to second-degree murder.

Henry Lorenz, aged twenty-two, the younger and also the leader, was a tall blond German, born abroad. Harry Dwyer, aged twenty-seven, was a ruddy and curly-haired youth of French-Irish descent, also born abroad. Both had come to the United States when very young.

The pair came to El Paso on the first of November, three weeks before the robbery, and put up at a hotel on South El Paso Street. While living at this hotel they bought cowboy boots and hats, and also cow-ponies and bridles and saddles. They made frequent trips between El Paso and Deming, and on one occasion brought back with them two girls. These girls knew they were going to hold up the train, apparently, and waited for them to return to El Paso after the affair was over.

Henry, the German boy, was supported at the trial by the presence of his sister Margaret and his father. The old man held a shabby Bible, and his lips mumbled prayers. Harry had no relatives with him, but he held in his hands a letter from his mother in Canada. She wrote him that she and his eight brothers and sisters were praying for him; it was all they could do, for they had no money to send for his defense.

A well-known newspaperwoman of Las Cruces, Margaret Page Hood, attended the trial and fell into talk with Henry's sister. Margaret Lorenz told her that Henry was really a good boy, but he had always been crazy about the West.

"I loved him best of the family, for he was my baby brother," she said. "He was born in a detention camp in Germany. Father had taken us to Russia to settle on a farm colony, but after the war broke out we were sent back to Germany and had no place to go but the camp. Mother died, and I took care of Henry. Pretty soon we came to America, and were happy and could go to school."

But the father married again, and the stepmother took a dislike to Henry. Henry sneaked western magazines to bed with him to read after the others had gone to sleep, although his father had forbidden him to do so. He spent whatever money he earned on western movies. He kept teasing his father for high-heeled boots and a big hat.

"So finally he ran away. For a long time I didn't hear from him, and then one day I got a letter saying he was working and saving his money to go West."

Margaret Lorenz was a stenographer and it was her slender savings that paid the way for her and her father to come to Henry's side.

Henry had saved five hundred dollars working in a New York shoe store. He testified that he had always wanted to see the West. "So I said to my pal Harry, 'Come along, Harry, I'll stake you to a trip. We'll go West and be cowboys.'"

The five hundred dollars went fast after they met the girls. "Finally I sold our horses and saddles. I told Harry we'd go farther West. Maybe to Arizona or California. Perhaps we'd have better luck out there. We didn't have any money left, so we decided to hold up the train to get enough for the trip."

He said he hadn't intended to use his gun, except to frighten the passengers, but when he saw that Harry was in trouble he let fly.

Harry said in his thick Irish voice, "I'll spend all my life making up for it, sir, if you'll go easy on us."

And Henry said, "All I can say, sir, is I'm sorry. I didn't mean to do it. I didn't plan to kill anyone. It was an accident."

It is interesting that Henry had been able to save up five hundred dollars during the lean years when most people couldn't save a penny, that he shared it with a friend, that he saved it for so dubious a venture, and that he made it go as long as he did, including horses, saddles, and girls for two.

Judge Frenger, I imagine, could hardly help giving the boys such a stiff sentence. Public opinion had been roused by the newspapers. And Margaret Lorenz and her father had gone to see the widow and the consumptive daughter of the man Henry had slain, to express their grief. The widow was not impressed, and next day demanded an "eye for an eye" in the columns of the Las Cruces papers. And the eastern papers had played up the story all the more when it was discovered that the hold-up was not the work of "bad men," but of drugstore cowboys from New York.

Mrs. Hood had the excellent idea of writing up the

trial as an eye-witness, and I was able to publish her story on the *New Mexico Sentinel* literary page.

I borrow from Mrs. Hood's account the following postscript:

The morning after the trial she happened to take the bus to El Paso. Margaret Lorenz and her father were sitting across the aisle, and just as the bus started an acquaintance came in and sat down beside her. When they neared the turn-off to Old Mesilla, he jogged Mrs. Hood's arm to attract her attention, and pointed to a new roadside sign, advertising the Billy the Kid Museum, three miles.

"Catch the eyes of plenty of tourists, that will, and get them to stop over. They have Billy the Kid's leg-irons and one of his guns over there."

"Yes," Mrs. Hood answered, "it ought to catch them —the tourists and all the silly kids back East who are led to believe that lawlessness is still romance."

"What's eating you?" he inquired.

She motioned across the aisle. The old man was still mumbling and holding his Bible, and Margaret's cheeks were wet.

"Oh, yes," he agreed. "Too bad. But imagine those young scoundrels thinking they could come out here and pull Wild West stuff on us."

There is now another Billy the Kid museum, the Lincoln County State Monument, in the beautiful old jail in Lincoln. It sits by the roadside, with the village trees about it, in the calm peaceful valley so much like many valleys back in New York and Pennsylvania that it is hard to believe it was once the scene of the bloody Murphy-McSween feud. So far this new museum has few exhibits that deal directly with the Kid, except for the books about him, which are growing rapidly in number. I recently sent John Sinclair, the young writer who is the curator of the museum, Mrs. Hood's account of the trial of the young men who imitated the Kid in the hold-up at Mt. Riley, suggesting a museum file under the heading, "Results of Hero-Worshiping William Bonney."

22. The Canyon

After three days Captain Melgosa and one Juan Galeras and another companion, the three lightest and most agile men, made an attempt to go down. They returned about four o'clock in the afternoon, not having succeeded in reaching the bottom. They said they had been down about a third of the way, and that the river seemed very large. Those who stayed above had guessed some huge rocks on the sides of the cliffs might be about as tall as a man, but those who went down swore that when they reached those rocks they were bigger than the great tower of Seville in Spain.

—Castañeda's *Narrative of the Coronado Expedition*

BIGGER than the great tower of Seville; the first response by white men to the Grand Canyon of the Colorado. The Spaniard could be vivid when he was startled. Take another phrase from Castañeda, "The country was so flat you could see the sky under the belly of a horse."

The Canyon is beyond a human being's range of response. We can say vivid things, even poetic things, but they make a curious collection when you see a group of them (a little book of things people have said has been printed). I visited the Canyon first by rail, and the porter told me of his first sight of it.

198

"I took my head in my hands and walked back and forth, moaning, 'How come that big hole thar?' "

Witter Bynner once told me that at his first sight of it he thanked heaven for the relief of an indifferent blue jay wheeling over the depths. Count Hermann Keyserling in *The Travel Diary of a Philosopher* was reminded of something Kant had said, and a few pages later is not sure that he agrees with whatever it was Kant said, for after all Kant had never seen the Canyon. A Chicago business executive took a single look from his hotel window, then pulled down the shade, and never lifted it again while he was there.

The extent to which erosion will go is terrifying. This colored panorama of destruction was caused by a not very big stream carrying silt and pebbles. There is a tiny petrified crab in a case in the museum at Yavapai Point. It was disturbed thousands of feet down, uncovered thousands of years later, by the river. But it is perfect. Lucky crab, to be in evidence at all; we shan't be—that reflection is bound to come to everyone who sees it, I suppose. And as one is sure to have a number of such reflections, bearing on man against the cosmos, I think of the Canyon as first of all an exercise for the intelligence.

Most sensitive persons wherever you meet them are still deep in *Weltschmerz*. The way the Southwest helps is not its remoteness from the crowded places of our age, as Easterners seem to think. Nothing is remote any longer. You can leave New York at dusk and have breakfast at your dude ranch in New Mexico or Arizona the next morning. What the Southwest does is to remind you constantly of the great age of the earth and the brief span, so far, of the human race.

Once I was talking to Erna Fergusson about the Canyon. She knows it gives me a kind of seasickness and sleeplessness—what I call cosmic vertigo. But she also knows that I go to see it whenever I can. I asked her how she herself handled such a spectacle. She gave me the exact answer I was after. She told me about hearing James Harvey Robinson give the lectures that went into that fine book *The Mind in the Making:*

"Here was a man who thought history should include all human experience, so we could understand the present and deal with it better.

"He did something I've never forgotten. He showed us a clock dial to illustrate human culture on this planet. He allowed twelve hours for the whole show, with today as high noon. That meant our civilization began in Egypt only twenty minutes ago. The Greeks precede us by only seven minutes. Scarcely half a minute has passed since the invention of the steam engine showed that starvation and slavery could be brought to an end.

"It makes it seem foolish to shed tears over the ineptitudes of us babies not yet out of human kindergarten. Maybe not yet even admitted to our kindergarten."

The Canyon, I think, lectures you to much the same effect as Dr. Robinson. You are forever hearing people say that Congress and the President should be made to visit it once a year. Hitler would have been a vastly different man, too, if he had only seen the Canyon. All Americans should be required by law to see it while they are still young and impressionable. Their way should be paid if necessary. Americans need to experience the feeling of time the Canyon gives. We are too much in a hurry. We have funny ambitions. This is the way people talk about the Canyon; they feel it as educational, and able to improve you. If they don't come away obviously improved themselves, and go home and start being better citizens, still they have registered a moral shock of some kind.

Probably we need hope more than the Vitamin B or Haliver oil pills nearly everybody who can afford them takes today. This hope really lives in a lot of little things we are feeling even if we are still in our prekindergarten stage—for example, that we don't like pleasures other people are debarred from because they are sick, or poor, or handicapped. A feeling like that, which comes out in Whitman and Emerson and other American writers, is working inside us in its molecular way, to help build the new world of man. Many things can cause it in us, and among them is certainly the sight of the Canyon. It debunks the ego like nothing else.

Many people make a pilgrimage to the Canyon every year. Once I went there with Gustave Baumann, stopping along the way at the near-by Painted Desert country and the Blue Forest. Those devastated areas are like a million butterflies fluttering in the luminous air, over debris of tortoise-shell. They are like a million leopards leaping on a million zebras in a world of opal. And they are an exceedingly cold world of geometry in which for millions of years the rhomboid has pertained to the parallelogram, and neither to anything else. Utterly irrelevant, and utterly beautiful.

I said to Baumann, "It isn't a million painted butterflies, it's a million gray-blue rhinoceroses of the Heroic-Romantic-Ego ages, perished in a bunch here."

"Looks to me like a New England barnyard turned to stone," he answered.

We got out of the car and took a long saunter down below in the great basin. Red trunks were severed from red thighs, and the heads also lay apart. Gray seaweed or hair comes down from the tops of the mounds. Those shapes—"elephant's guts," Baumann called them, those kidney and liver shapes.

The rhomboid keeps on addressing the parallelogram in ambiguous color. Miles away on the horizon the high blue heads of mesas rest on sloping shoulders till the mirage guillotines them. Convoluting clouds trail like spray or hair. Where there is only sand very little can grow. Even the sagebrush quits at last, leaving it to the clouds to do something.

Near Lee's Ferry we saw the first signs of the Canyon. We came to a place where everything was parallel and long shadows from the clouds streaked the buttes and brought out unsuspected forms. Baumann began to talk about the Canyon, the nightmare of it from a painter's point of view.

"You see a wonderful composition and when you look back again, it's gone. See how fast those clouds are moving.

"This is the reason nobody can paint the Canyon. There was a fellow came out from Chicago some years ago. He had an eight-foot canvas-stretcher in his car. He said he *knew* he could paint the Canyon.

" 'Have you ever seen it?' I asked him.

" 'No,' he said.

" 'Then take your stretcher and start right back to Chicago.'

"He thought I was trying to keep the Canyon to myself. But four months later he came back. He had his picture, of course, but it was no good, just like everybody else's. He said he kept seeing swell compositions and losing them. He was tired and a little frightened.

"Then there was a woman about ten years ago. At first she did some very nice things, seized little parts of the living country; but she soon grew tired battling with the shadows, and used to sit quietly by a tree and paint the tree."

Last year my wife and I stayed at the Canyon several days. We walked the rim at night, saw the moon come up and drop long streaks of silver and jet into the depths. I could feel no feeling, for I was all chronology, zoology, geology, geometry, algebra, and astronomy. Those outer worlds where I am not at ease captured me. But I broke free the moment we took the road homeward. We decided to return via Flagstaff. Flagstaff is a grove of pine trees, but it has houses under the pines, and a good many babies and dogs.

At the Canyon we had looked through telescopes at the earth laid bare for a mile below us. At Flagstaff we visited Dr. Colton's Museum, which sits in a prayerful attitude at the foot of the San Francisco peaks. Those peaks tower a mile in the air and are framed in the great windows at the end of the museum hall. Dr. Colton has spent a pious and useful life, really wonderful, making charts of the strata of the peaks and getting examples of birds, trees, flowers, and stones from each stratum. We saw these charts in the museum.

I admire Dr. Colton out of the ordinary. At the same time, I believe a day will come when a man will build a museum in an ordinary little town, perhaps in Texas, or Kansas even, deprived of everything spectacular, but sitting on the old earth nonetheless, and perhaps beside a quite ordinary and uninteresting dry river or creek, with some scraggly cottonwoods on the banks. And this museum will be filled with the common things one might find in any field—yet, touched by the right kind of science and the right kind of religion, they will be absorbingly interesting and revealing.

Something of this sort could happen, and perhaps in a small way is happening, to history and biography, domains generally consecrated to the celebration of the ego. But that is something yet again, as Baumann says.

23. People Lost

The near tragedy . . . at the ice cave in Valencia County
may lead to the closing of the famous phenomenon. . . . Said
Governor Tingley, "There is no marked or visible trail to it
from the highway. The few signs that were there have been
knocked down. The cave itself is unsafe; the ladders are dilapi-
dated. . . ."

—*Albuquerque*, New Mexico, *Journal*, July 31, 1938

I T WOULD be impossible even with federal aid to
make safe for tourists every place of interest along
the highways of Arizona and New Mexico. The two
states are doing pretty well, I think, considering the
nature of the land, and the nature of tourists.

Marie Antoinette de Laforrest, a twenty-one-year-
old girl from Vannes, France, came to Kentucky in
1937 on a student permit, and tutored French in Lex-
ington. With her aunts, Irene Piedalue, a home demonstration agent of Winchester, Kentucky, and Laura
Piedalue, a New York social worker, she set out on a
motor trip to the West coast in early July, 1938.

At six o'clock Tuesday morning, July 26, they
checked out of the El Fidel Hotel in Albuquerque, and

took the road west after a hasty breakfast. It was their last food for four days. They had heard of the ice cave and turned off the main highway southwest of Grants to see it. The landscape here is grand but lonely and desolate. The cave is located at the base of the Zuñi mountains, and on the edge of the San Mateo malpais, or lava beds. They found the highway marker for the cave, and left their car by the roadside.

Fortunately for them, a rancher drove up the dirt road that noon and noticed the parked car. Two days later he drove back down the road and saw the car still there. When he reached his ranch he telephoned the State Police. Governor Tingley himself led the search. Early Saturday morning he was on the ground with the troopers, forest service men, and CCC workers. They first explored the caves, with flashlights and ropes, and during this episode the Governor got himself onto a perch and had to be rescued by those below him.

As the women were not in the caves, the party mobilized for a dragnet search of the region. CCC boys and volunteers, spaced twenty feet apart and directed by troopers and forest men, with State Hunter Homer Pickens and his bear hounds also at hand, scoured the malpais on a mile-wide front, swinging in a circle southward. Three hours later boys from San Fidel and Cubero came upon the lost women. They were lying in the limited shade of a piñon, exhausted but not at all hysterical. Laura Piedalue drew out her rosary, kissed it, and exclaimed, "God bless you, boys."

Their shoes were in better condition than one would expect, after the razor-edged volcanic rock. But their dresses were in ribbons, and Marie Antoinette, who was wearing split skirt, shorts and blouse, had badly sunburned legs. All three were scratched and spotted with pitch.

Marie Antoinette drew two balls of resin from inside her blouse. "Zis is all we have to eat," she said, throwing them away. "Last night it rain. We take pine needles and suck zem like zis to drink. But we do not get enough to drink. Only to moisten ze lips."

The three had kept their heads. Laura Piedalue said, "We saw the big hole with ladders, but we were so disappointed we started back to the car. We had been led to believe the ice cave was something wonderful. Then we just couldn't find the path. We were frantic, but we soon calmed down and tried to proceed in orderly fashion. We kept moving so we wouldn't get stiff. At night we took turns keeping watch. We never lost hope that someone would find us."

The women were carried to the Governor's automobile, and were soon in Albuquerque where they could rest and repair themselves. People of New Mexico took satisfaction in their dining at the Governor's Mansion the following day. It is awkward when a guest in your house has a bad time of it.

There are always items in the newspapers about lost people. On April 18 of 1940 a young Navajo girl named Napah was recovering in the Tohatchi, Arizona, hospital from the effects of four days of wandering in the northern desert region of the reservation. She was found dazed at a point one hundred miles from where she disappeared. She had apparently walked almost steadily. Sheepherders had seen her from a distance at various points during the long walk, but had not taken the trouble to investigate. It is strange too that the girl had not gone in their direction. In that vast land it may be that she had not seen them, or it may be that she was afraid.

On April 3, Charles Keith Childers, a two-and-a-half-year-old boy, wandered away from the house of his grandmother at Rincona, New Mexico, about noon, with his shepherd dog. When night came, an unusually cold night for the time of year, he had not returned. His grandmother, Mrs. Simms, notified the troopers, and they came with bloodhounds. Fifty Rincona residents joined the search, and they came on the boy before dawn, "awfully cold" but unharmed. He owed his life to the insistent barking of his dog, which led a trooper to him.

On May 29 a posse of rangers were searching the Eel River canyon country for Mrs. Doris Thompson, a woman of forty. It was believed that she had wandered

into the mountains to die. I saw no record in the papers
later of her being rescued. Mrs. Thompson's four-year-
old son Teddy was frozen to death in 1938. He had
been mute since birth but was just learning to speak.
His mother spanked him for throwing his knife and
spoon on the floor after breakfast. Teddy ran away.
Two months later his body was found huddled under
a bush two miles from home, and only a few feet from
a path traveled by scores of searchers. He had apparently frozen on his first night in the forest.

On May 28 Janet Retallack, two and a half years
old, wandered away from her parents' cabin on Tur-
quoise Lake, in the Central Rockies, a little west of
Leadville. She was found the next day at dawn. "She
was lying down but was not asleep, and far from being
frightened was the calmest one of the bunch," said a
searcher.

On April 5, Mrs. Bessie Bowman, a woman of seventy, spent five days in the mesquite of the Mexicali
desert. She had gone to the border with a party of four
on an amateur prospecting trip, and became separated
from the others. A Mexican posse found her munching
cactus leaves. Mrs. Bowman, a white woman, said she
was a disciple of Father Divine, the Negro leader, and
had been hired by the others to help them locate gold
and silver in the desert. "I had no fear while I was
lost," she said. "A spirit told me I would live for eight-

een days but that I would be found before then. The spirit informed me of this so clearly that I had no doubt it was true."

An unusual adventure of this kind happened last November to a seven-year-old boy of Winslow, Arizona, named Bruce Crozier. Bruce disappeared Sunday morning from a hunting camp sixty miles south of Winslow, wearing a light playsuit and new boots, and no coat. A week later lacking seventeen hours, he walked into another camp thirty-two miles in a straight line from the place of his disappearance. He had been given up as dead by the searchers after the fourth night, for nobody expected him to survive freezing temperatures without food and shelter. Experienced Navajo trackers, bloodhounds, and hunting dogs were put on his trail, but no one caught a glimpse of him.

Bruce walked into a small clearing the second Sunday of his being lost, and sat down on the running board of a car. The owners of the car found him on their return from hunting deer. He asked them for a drink of water.

"Are you lost?"

"I wouldn't want to be lost any worse," he replied. "I was far enough in the woods this time."

The hunters guessed they were talking to the child whose disappearance had been disturbing three states.

They took him to the Heber ranch, and then to the hospital at Holbrook, forty-five miles distant.

Dr. R. L. Davis of Holbrook attended Bruce. He found him suffering from "severe exhaustion and dehydration" but would not commit himself as to how much longer Bruce might have held out. "Through some miracle," he said, "the boy's general condition is quite good." It makes you wonder about a number of things.

The firmest institutions of society are those grouped about children, to protect them during their period of growth and train them to endure the strains of adult life. We do not regard children as capable of enduring much. We know too well that they cannot do so. Yet here is a seven-year-old boy no better than naked in a light summer suit, exposed for a week to November weather, thirst, starvation, fear, and loneliness in a particularly wild stretch of country, and he comes through the experience.

Bruce told the hunters that he traveled only by day. "I figured I was already lost bad enough without trying to find my way around at night. When there was a cave I slept in it. If there wasn't a cave, I found a boulder, and heaped up a pile of leaves to lie down on and put on top of me."

"Weren't you afraid?"

"The first two nights I was. After that I wasn't."

I am inclined to wonder whether even the first two

nights Bruce felt much fear. He said nothing of any panic when he first knew he was lost. I was once lost myself in a northern Minnesota forest, though for less than twenty-four hours; and I have not forgotten my first rush of terror. But Bruce's remark to the men who found him, "I was far enough in the woods this time," suggests that he was out for an adventure. Even at seven a boy knows about Kit Carson and other scouts. Whatever the cause, fear did not damage his chance for survival. And he had a plan of campaign of his own, to stay put at night and make sure of as much shelter and warmth as possible.

The human body is a device for resisting stress. Under stress most of the time, it does not stay rigid and wear out, but changes its tactics to meet each new danger. The purpose of this endless secret strategy is to keep the individual alive as long as possible. So the body is above all an instrument of adaptation. This is a business both intraorganic and extraorganic, both physical and psychic. In Bruce Crozier these adjustments took place with a maximum of reinforcement for him. Bruce is an individual. He was at this time an individual lost for seven days. You cannot consider him identical with any other boy of his age lost for the same length of time, or with anybody else in the same plight.

Some people die if lost overnight. Two woodcutters of Cienega, one old and one young, died while lost a few hours in a September storm of wet snow. A ten-year-old Armijo boy, named Juan Gurule, missing for less than two days in clement May weather, was found dead, apparently from exposure, in a cottonwood bosque a few miles from Belen. You never know whether lost people will die or survive. And for the reason that lostness is a different fact to each and all called upon to face it.

If we are born and die one by one, it is also one by one that we must adapt, and not by thousands and millions. But our fellows do come into the picture, and with tremendous weight. They play their part beforehand. In great degree they determine for us our chances of adapting. Collectively they control our physical condition, whether we have been housed and fed well, and protected in our growing up. They are responsible in part certainly for our attitude towards life, whether it is courageous or despairing. Fear in children must often be due to home influence, and Bruce's father and mother, obviously, had brought him up to the ripe age of seven blessedly fearless. Inquiry might bring to light to a religious training of the good sort that banishes terror. Lack of fear is sometimes due to lack of imagination; but in Bruce's case it seems a positive imagination that led him into getting his fill of the woods. Finally, and perhaps most important, Bruce was in good health. His father, the manager of a Winslow store, had a steady job, could provide for his family, and put a roof over their heads. The two

Cienega woodcutters did not enter their battle with the brief snowstorm well prepared physically. It is plain they died of fright, whatever that implies to a doctor. I know nothing of the Armijo ten-year-old boy who died in a cottonwood bosque near a large town; some essential was lacking, the lack of it cut him off. The three Frenchwomen who had to endure four days of the lava beds were in sound health mentally and physically, had steady jobs, and were supported by religious faith. They were also supported by one another's presence. Loneliness breeds phantoms, but companionship reminds us of our code of life and of death.

The following story has a different point. A party of Easterners entered the Navajo reservation, two men and two women, and one of the men strayed away from the car and got himself thoroughly lost. His friends were much concerned, and lost no time in spreading word. The other man said he would give a reward for his safe return. A Navajo boy offered his services as a tracker. But he specified a much larger reward than the man had offered; he said, "Give me $3,000 and I'll find him." It seemed a high value for a simple Indian boy to put upon his services, but the man could afford it, and he agreed.

The Indian boy asked the party to accompany him, so that they might see his prowess as a tracker. He was able to follow the lost man's imprints in the sand, though they were five days old. He would stop and say, "Here the man felt very sick," or, "Here the man saw a big rattlesnake, and was very scared." Or, "Here the man turned his ankle. Very hard for him to go on. He sit on this stone." The boy was so graphic in delineating the experience of the man who was lost that it made the people wretched, and they returned to camp to wait. They got to wondering about the boy, and the women thought he was enjoying himself too much.

So the party telegraphed the F.B.I. for help. Two detectives arrived the same evening. They were amused when they learned what was going on, and the size of the fee the boy had demanded. The next morning before dawn the detectives stole out of camp, leaving word for the party to wait for them. They went straight to the boy's hogan, or home. And there they found the missing man, in good condition except for a sprained ankle. He had been there three days. The Navajo boy explained that for a long time he had wanted to go to Washington, D. C., to law school. But he saw no way of getting the money. Then this man came wandering to his hogan, and the boy perceived that the gods were coming to his assistance. He assured the man that he would get in touch with his friends. He assured the friends that for $3,000 he would find the man.

The federal agents told the other man that since he had been duped he would not need to pay up. But the boy's mental processes interested him, and so did his ambition to become a lawyer. The man was a lawyer himself. He said it was worth $3,000 to him to be made a sucker of by a young Navajo, and he gave the boy the money.

24. The Cavern

Tourist travel through the Carlsbad Caverns fell a little short last month, but it was the third successive April in which more than 11,000 persons saw the underground wonders.

—Las Cruces, New Mexico, Sun-News, May 2, 1940

THE CARLSBAD CAVERNS are an event of inward and outward living in a different way from the Grand Canyon. Other visitors to the Canyon at the time you are there can hardly matter much to you. You do not brush elbows with them; most of them you do not even see, and those you do see you are not likely to see twice. They come by train, and stay a day or so, or they come by car, and are off again in an hour or so, or when they please. The Canyon is something you have to face by yourself. Only a tiny proportion of visitors descend the trail through the heaped-up temples and towers of colored earth. The rest of the tourists take the Canyon through their eyes and generally through colored glasses. The Canyon is a somewhat formal affair, too. The scenic views are along forest boulevards or stone walks that seem to have been there a long time, and all the buildings melt into the time-lessness of the fir groves that envelop them. There is a great hush, and a great air of decorum, as though an important personage had just died. As a young man said, you see the Canyon in a top hat.

This loneliness and formality and sense of being cut off from the comforts of your kind help make the Canyon a deep experience. The Cavern can be as deep an experience, but you do not continue on your way thinking only of the fantasia of substance under the surface of the earth. You have in mind also the people you went underground with, for they give you as much cause for thought as the stalactites and stalagmites. Going through the Cavern is a folk festival. You must be at the Cavern at a set time, and become part of a group of hundreds of people; and with this party, under the eye of the rangers, take a walk of six subterranean miles. In the course of descending, ascending, hurrying, pausing, sauntering, sidling, you stop for a forty-five-minute luncheon at a cafeteria in an enormous and well-lighted chamber. If you aren't acquainted with a dozen or so people by now, it will happen here, or else what a pity.

The approach to the entrance of the Cavern is all that it should be. You reach the summits of the wide hills by a valley from the plains, full of bare boulders of limestone and bushes with metallic green leaves that whisper gently of hell. The small yucca gives way to the joshua tree, which is a success in the way of psychic disturbance, and then bands of ocotillas appear, insanely beckoning you this way and that with long green arms on which grow tiny leaves like the leaves of trees. The heat is so intense on a July morning that you know if you were stripped of your clothes on those slopes you would be singing your swan song in five minutes.

You can go to the Grand Canyon by train, but not to the Cavern. I remember that the Brothers in charge of a boys' school in Santa Fe once wrote back to the headquarters of their order in France for permission to hire a 'bus, to take the boys to Carlsbad. Their superiors replied that it would be better for the boys to go on bicycles. The brothers had forgotten to tell the French priests that from Santa Fe the distance is 350 miles, with stretches of thirty and forty miles without house or water. I doubt whether anybody ever bicycles to Carlsbad or to the Grand Canyon, or walks to them, either. These spots are not on the knapsack routes. Even the nearest towns are too far away. It is a pity. Properly there should be a lack of ease about a pilgrimage; shrines should offer a certain difficulty, it is only right. But most of the meccas in the Southwest are so many miles away from anywhere that it seems funny; only the motorist can go, and if it is a dirt road, he may well go in fear and trembling.

This condition which seems suitable to a pilgrimage,

that it should not be a bed of roses, is met at the Cavern from the time you get out of your car. To begin with you do a great deal of waiting. You wait while standing in line at the information and ticket windows, in the scorching sun of that hill-top. Then you wait with your kind on the curving stone terraces of the path, until the appointed hour. You have time to get acquainted with a few near-by souls. If you came up at sunset the evening before to witness the night flight of the bats, and to hear the ranger lecturing about them, you probably have already struck up acquaintances. The ranger poised himself on a rock at some distance from his audience, but the air was clear and I am sure I heard him say there were between three and five million bats, and that they ate each night between eight and eleven tons of insects, within a circle of 150 miles. These facts seem to me as fantastic as what I later saw in the Cavern.

Every day the year round people come, hundreds of them, in every kind of dress, of every age, in every sort of car, from every state, from foreign lands, and they all can produce $1.50 to get in.

We were discussing why we had come, a group of Americans who had just met.

"I always wanted to see the Cavern," said a young man from the Texas oil fields. He had been paid the Saturday before, and was on a two weeks' vacation. He was with two other boys from the oil country, and one of them owned the car, and had enough money on his person to get all three safely home. They were in their shirtsleeves.

There were four girls from Grand Rapids, school-teachers, who had been on the road a month and were now returning home from the West coast. So far the trip had cost them thirty-five dollars apiece, because they did their own cooking.

"We wanted to see the West, and this is one of the high points of it," explained the talkative member. "I think this is going to be a thrill. We are going to the Mammoth Cave too, but that will be an anticlimax. It's been a wonderful trip. I hate to go home again."

"I wouldn't dare go home to Houston without seeing the Cavern," said a young man making up to the talkative girl. "What would they think? Everyone in Houston has been to the Cavern, and that's the first question they ask you."

A man who was with his wife and two young children said, "I'd give a penny to know why I am here."

A thirteen-year-old schoolgirl with black pigtails said, "People like to see things and see them together." Her eyes reminded me of dark shining birds.

The young man with her, in his bare arms but carrying a prudent wool jacket, said, "Isn't it the old wish to make a pilgrimage? We can't kill off those old wishes. We are full of them. They stick. But now it's the twentieth century and we're Americans, so when we go on a pilgrimage we go in our cars."

He was a hotel clerk on his vacation.

"You've got to go somewhere," said the oil-field boy.

"Won't you be cold?" I asked him.

"I'm so hot I'd just as soon be cold. I didn't even bother to take my coat out of the car."

When we first entered the Cavern the air at 56 degrees seemed quite chilly, but I suppose you adjust to it soon, if you are a young furnace. For a while people looked attentively at nature's marvels. But it is impossible to be overcome by anything very long, and talking recommenced, low talking. There were a dozen rangers along, ready to answer questions. One ranger gave a talk about what happens when water seeps through limestone, and everybody was interested and listened. The ranger also asked us to obey orders and not touch anything or stray from the path. The crowd seemed well enough behaved, and I doubt whether anyone would have strayed from the path under any circumstances.

He said too that Governor Miles had just brought a cavalcade of 'buses full of school-children to the Cavern, and the government let them through free. He told the schoolteachers to come back with their children and it wouldn't cost them a thing. That offer was a move in the right direction, but if you lived a long way from the Cavern it would cost a lot of money to bring even one 'busload of children. That is the real problem. All school-children in the country ought to see Carlsbad. It belongs to them, and is part of their education.

Detective William Martin went into the Cavern once for a fugitive from justice. The man, who was a murderer, went down with the crowd and stayed down. His idea was to hide overnight and come up to the surface with the tourists the next day. Martin and two officers followed him with gasoline lamps. They called him, and kept calling, and whether it was the disturbing echoes or his terror from being alone in the utter dark, he soon came running to give himself up. He cried, "Put me in jail—then I'll know where I am!"

It would be cold and clammy, but perhaps you could stick it out down there overnight with a good light and a good novel. This poor fellow had neither, and maybe a bad conscience.

The place is so well illuminated for the tourists' visit that the usual fear people have of being underground is absent. The vistas are extraordinary. I liked particularly watching the hundreds of human beings coming down the circling paths. The Cavern is well ventilated in an unknown way, but the smoke from cigarettes and pipes takes a while to clear out, and hangs in a gray pall at a distance. You see the people through it. It's like a dream out of Dante or Doré.

As we came up out of the earth, a woman of middle age told me she had visited the Cavern once before, with a man of eighty and his wife, who was very nearly that age.

"He had been in this neighborhood as a boy," she said, "and had gone about a lot on horseback. He often rode by the entrance of the Cavern and wished he could go in. He went back East and grew up, and time passed, and at last came the news that the government had made it possible for people to enter the Cavern and walk six of the thirty-five underground miles. This man kept talking to his wife about it, and at last they decided to go when they had a chance. Several years later the chance came. We spent the night at Carlsbad, and the old lady was so tired from the motor trip that she fainted on the hotel stairway. We didn't see how she could stand the Cavern if she couldn't stand the trip. But she had her mind made up. We got a doctor, and then we got in touch with a park service official. He was an understanding man, and he saw it was important that those two old people should be given their heart's desire. So, when we got to the cave entrance, we found that he had assigned special guides to take care of them. These guides practically carried the old lady through the part of the Cavern we saw. We didn't make the complete descent, but we went down far enough. I never saw such reverence and such delight, both at once, as those two old people had on their faces."

I was thinking about that story when I first caught sight of the daylight again. As I approached it, it seemed a sickly green, but when I came close to it and stepped into it, it changed to a most beautiful light, unbelievably rich and pure. I was glad the old couple, too, could have had that experience. It seemed to me the most vivid of the whole journey. As we have nothing to compare the sun with, we have no way of knowing the wonder of it.

25. Peyote

Stringent penalties were decreed by the Navajo tribal council today for use of the narcotic peyote weed, the Indian equivalent of the poppy and marijuana.

Action followed an investigation by Howard Gorman, vice
chairman of the council, who reported Indians used it in orgies
under the guise of religious rites.

A resolution was also prepared for presentation to congress
asking federal control of traffic in the weed. New Mexico statutes exist covering the drug but enforcement has not been
effective.

—*Farmington*, New Mexico, *Times-Hustler*

T HE PEYOTE religion is of real concern to many mid-
western tribes, but I had never heard much of it
among the Navajo and did not know what to make of
this report. The Navajo doubtless came to their tribal
council to talk about stock reduction and grazing regulations, matters immediately vital to their well-being.
Those in charge of the meeting introduced other topics
that might occupy them for a considerable portion if
not all of the scheduled meeting of three days. Dr.
Ruth Murray Underhill, who from all I hear knows as
much about it as anybody, feels that Indians do not
argue as white people do, for a decision on a matter;

that their aim is rather to reach harmony, and toward
this end everyone present desires to make his personal
contribution. Peyote thus occupied them an entire day.
Some say it was a problem better for them not to discuss publicly at all, since their medicine men were privately at work upon it.

Howard Gorman, a Navajo himself but also a Christian missionary, showed that peyote had come to an
outlying section of the tribe from contact with the
Utes. The Navajo bootleggers had clashed with priests
of the Ute peyote cult, and the Utes killed some of
them and stamped out the illegal liquor traffic. When
the Navajo herders drove their herds back from Utah
they brought peyote with them. Its growing use on the
reservation, according to Gorman, has caused family
dissensions. It is not hard to believe, especially in cases
where one of a married couple joins the cult and the
other does not. He charged, too, that peyote made
public nuisances of some of its takers, and people of
uncertain equilibrium might well perform actions like
holy-rolling while under its influence.

Gorman said that peyote was habit-forming, but
scientific evidence does not support this assertion.
Above all he held it responsible for lewd conduct.
Scientific opinion makes this charge unlikely also. He
introduced charges of immorality in several sworn
statements, among them one by a seventeen-year-old
Navajo girl. She swore that she and a girl friend had

left a peyote meeting at Jimmy Thompson's hogan, and young men had followed them. "Both of us were under the influence of peyote. Men passed remarks that they wanted to lay down with us. I will never attend another peyote meeting." It might be mentioned that Navajo girls do not generally leave hogans at night (or at any time) without the protection of an older woman.

Many of those present at the council had never heard of peyote before, and they were naturally alarmed. The council voted a fine of $100 and six months in prison for any member of the tribe taking peyote.

At this time Maria Chabot came back from the reservation and I had a talk with her. The New Mexico Association on Indian Affairs had sent her there to find out how the Navajo liked the New Deal. She was also collecting Navajo silver and weaving for the Pitt Rivers museum of Oxford. Miss Chabot is a thoughtful young woman who looks like a Madonna by one of the Dutch masters. She is a student of native peoples under white domination, and knows about such matters as French colonial administration in Algeria and Tunisia, and recent developments in the treatment of natives in the various British colonies. She had spent a good deal of time among the Navajo before, and had just traveled some two thousand miles on the reservation.

Howard Gorman, the Navajo missionary who had

taken evidence on peyote, had for many years been
eager, it seemed, to persuade a young Navajo named
Dooley Shorty to go to missionary school. Hosteen
(Mr.) Shorty resisted his arguments. He hoped to be
a medicine man, and had already learned some three
hundred of the eleven hundred songs of one of the
Nine Day Chants. Of late he had become interested in
the peyote religion.

Maria Chabot told me that Hosteen Shorty felt
badly about being on the list of young men condemned
by the council. She was at the time driving an unusual
contraption somewhat like a motor prairie-schooner,
but a few miles away at Gallup she knew of a high-
powered car she could borrow. When she heard what
had happened she went to his home, and suggested
that he go for a ride with her. Maria and Shorty drove
many miles that night and said many things to one another about the mystery of existence, God, religion,
human nature, missionaries, and tribal customs among
both palefaces and redskins. What a young woman
sympathetic to native peoples and yet studying them
objectively, and a young man training for the medicine craft and caught along the way by enthusiasm for
peyote, might confide in one another on such a night
would be worth hearing, I'm sure. I did not feel entitled to know and did not ask her; I prefer to think of
all such talks, which the vast spaces of this region

breed even between strangers, as going out of the recesses of their souls, and away from them among the little piñones and sabinas, to be lost in eternity.

But what Maria did say of their talk was interesting. She pointed out to Shorty the difficulties that lay ahead of him, and inquired:

"Will you give up peyote because of the council?"

"No."

"You come of medicine men and are studying to be one yourself. Why did you join peyote?"

"My people do not believe in the old religion any more."

"What does your grandfather say?"

Shorty's grandfather is an eminent figure among his people.

"I showed him the peyote button. He said, 'Anything is a medicine if you do it right, if you believe in it.'"

Apparently Navajo shamans can have a catholicity and religious sophistication difficult to find in any caste or priesthood. Little by little as he aged, the old man must have shut out of his remembrance all that was not of love, all the landmarks of dogmatism and self-righteousness, of sloth and crabbedness. But retaining what was of love, he could welcome this crude boy his grandson into his own wide world, transmuted by pity and by clairvoyance as to what persists where so much changes.

Peyote is not a weed, as the news item says, but the button of a small cactus which grows abundantly along the lower Rio Grande near Laredo. Nor is it the Indian equivalent of the poppy and the marijuana. The Indians, at least the medicine men, know marijuana, man's ancient and unfriendly friend hasheesh, made of the hemp plant. It has no hold on them, just as it has no hold on the Chinese, who have had it from time immemorial. Peyote is something yet again and more interesting.

The peyote button, when gathered and dried, has been used for centuries by Indians from Mexico City to the Arkansas River, to produce a certain mental exhilaration. The plains Indians say that this state, in the individual, is one of friendliness and well-being; in the group, of inter-tribal brotherhood. Thus various peyote "churches" have come into being. The most important of these, the First Born Church of Christ, was incorporated under the laws of Oklahoma in 1914. Perhaps to satisfy formal requirements, the name was later changed to the Native American Church, and this name it bears today.

From what you hear, peyote is taken at a ceremony which lasts throughout the night, and is accompanied by the beating of a small gourd rattle and a tiny ..ater drum. Slight noises intensify the visual impressions of the peyote-taker, and stir his imagination. The mingling of the alkaloids result in synesthesis, that is, per-

ception of items proper to one sense in terms of another. A subject of Havelock Ellis had a "curious sensation of tasting colors." Rouhier tells of an experiment
in which the sound of a bell became a "surréaliste ag-
gregate of flowing, pulsating lines." Dixon says of the
sound of a piano, "the whole air was filled with music,
each note of which seemed to arrange itself around a
medley of other notes . . . surrounded in turn by a
halo of color pulsating to the music."

Havelock Ellis tried peyote on himself, in the early
days of its scientific investigation. He thought its pleasure was not in the passive emotional states tea or alcohol produce, but strictly in the color visions. Others
say the state of mind it produces is as important as the
visions. Ellis goes on to say it impaired his attention
but not his judgment, and that in his memory the
visions remained beautiful. This is more the general
verdict.

The mature button contains nine different alkaloids.
The strychnine-like alkaloids take effect first, in physical and mental exhilaration. For this reason the ancient
Mexicans could use peyote just before foot-races and
battle. But the morphine-like alkaloids are bound to
come along and make you dreamy. That is, one group
of alkaloids increases reflex-irritability, while the other
is soporific. But what confuses their interaction is the
fact that ordinarily six or eight buttons are eaten or an
infusion of them drunk at intervals during the cere-

mony. You have no desire or ability to sleep for many hours after you have taken peyote.

A government bulletin gives the experience of Charles E. Shell, a white man. With a doctor in attendance, Mr. Shell took ten buttons, steeped in tepid water for twenty-five hours. The doctor, following him as he wandered about the garden, saw a young bird which had fallen from its nest. He got a rake and lifted the bird up into the nest again. Mr. Shell said afterwards of this deed, "It seemed to me the doctor was undertaking to bring about a universal brotherhood in the bird kingdom." He summed up the effect of peyote on him thus, "For the time being the millennium has come. . . . If these experiences could be made universal and continuous, there would be no need of armies, navies, or courts. . . ."

Dr. S. Weir Mitchell enjoyed taking peyote so much that he predicted "a perilous reign of the mescal habit when this agent becomes attainable." But Dr. Mitchell's fear is probably groundless. Peyote is too disagreeable to take, ever to become popular. When you first take it, it makes you retch or vomit; as the Indians say, "You must suffer to peyote." And its results are not uniform. E. B. Putt says he suffered acutely from the ticking of his watch. Weston La Barre, who has written an account of peyote, found that in an Oto meeting he had visions of animals so hilariously funny it was difficult to observe decorum; while in an experiment in New Haven in the shadow of Yale University, the "psychic state developed into one of stark, galloping, psychotic terror."

There is no scientific evidence that peyote is habit-forming. As to its being sexually stimulating, the evidence is decidedly the other way. It is also antagonistic to whiskey and strong drink. The two are not compatible in any mortal stomach, and peyote offers a superior attraction to drink addicts. At the tribal council at Window Rock, Hola Tsoi, for example, said that everyone present knew peyote had cured three outstanding drunkards (he mentioned them by name). He himself had renounced the use of alcohol because peyote required it of him.

The arguments brought to discredit the peyote cult make it appear likely that its critics misconceive its true significance. Far from being used for licentious reasons it is the recourse of those who have had all the license (and all the despair) they wish. It has its strongest hold on those young people who have been to Indian schools, and who as a result are pretty well uprooted. It is to those of the young who cannot believe in their tribal religions longer, that peyote comes as a way ahead. Christianity offers little or nothing to many of them; they see no chance of fitting into the U. S. American way of life. They have learned about birth control, and many are hard drinkers; and their life, vicious because unrelated and irresponsible, is not unlike the life of such young people anywhere. When you find nothing that seems worth striving for, you see no reason for the family or for bringing children into the world to continue the misery of life.

The interim religions that come while the older creeds are being readjusted to new needs and while what the future contains is still unknown, must attack first of all the notion that life is nothing but misery. In one way or another they must make new and shining the sanctity of the family, thinking in terms of children and their future, and the forms of mutual helpfulness concealed in an abstract term like brotherhood. Peyote is a religion of moon and of woman, of ecstatic visions, and of friends and acquaintances who come not from the boundaries of one tribe only, but from many tribes.

Congress has been urged on various occasions to control the traffic in the drug, and one bad part of the situation seems to be that commercially minded whites have tried to make a good thing of it, by selling it as a panacea for whatever ails one. Thus it was sold to Ute women as a kind of twilight sleep. The drug, being a depressant, results in temporary muscular paralysis in degrees varying according to the users, and may cause death in childbirth. But Congress has refrained from any stringent control of peyote, no doubt wisely. Weir Mitchell gave his opinion thus: "It is really a rather harmless drug as compared with most of the others which men use, and I think such a law quite ridiculous." Hrdlička, after a thorough investigation of peyote, concluded, "The drug can perhaps be likened to nicotine, and the latter will doubtless not affect different individuals to the same degree. . . . I should by no means join myself to those who see in it any *great* danger." Agreeing with this statement, Weston La Barre goes on to say in his study of peyote that "given the Plains religious and ideological background, the peyote cult is entirely plausible as a religion, and the issue is properly one of religious freedom."

Among the Pawnee, the leader closes the night-long meeting at noon with a lecture on ethical matters, speaking especially against the use of alcohol. The lecture is perhaps a general characteristic of primitive New World society; in the Pueblos of the Rio Grande, the head men have always been given to daily moral discourse. The tendency goes far back, but on the Plains it seems now associated closely with the peyote cult. One of the chief features of the peyote meetings is the public confession of sins. Public confession is also a widespread aboriginal pattern, with or without peyote; but to ask pardon of those one has wronged in the presence of the Father Peyote, gives the event special significance.

Watched and controlled as they are now, it is a matter of concern to Indian tribes to find some depth of life together. Yet here there is the greatest difficulty

because of that former religion of theirs, born out of
freedom in nature and worship of all things in a true
setting. With different ancestry and topography the
rituals differed among the tribes. What peyote is offering as a common refuge, apart from auditory and
visual hallucinations of a better life and the helpful and healing impulses which Christianity itself
preaches, is a quite fundamental worship of woman
and the family.

The Indians have always had their ethics, of course,
and their systems of healing; but what they excelled
in was worship—what *we* do not excel in, I am afraid.
To express what they felt about the beauty and wonder
of life they developed their very great art of dancing,
with the pantomime, costume (including jewelry and
feathers), and music that attend it. While we have
nothing in our past that even faintly resembles such
worship, we may have something like it inside us—
a desire to render thanks in ways integrated and fascinating and quite apart from singing hymns together
and listening to sermons. At least I have thought so,
as I observed young whites at Indian dances.

Among the Navajo and the Pueblos the older religions have been too dominating to allow of that con-
fusion and fear which is the base of the peyote cult;
and so, until lately, peyote has only the slightest place
in their annals. But peyotism would appear to be the
living religion of the majority of plains Indians today.

It functions as a complete religion: it baptizes the children and instructs them, marries young people, assists adults in improving their behavior, and buries the dead. Socially, it is a focus for intertribal as well as tribal life; many graduates of the government Indian schools travel a great deal, and they talk in the peyote meetings. The youthful Navajo appreciates the advantages of being in touch with his kind, pooling impressions of the New Deal, and formulating opinions and policies to withstand the successive shocks he is heir to as the ward of Washington. The peyote cult can best be understood by its attraction for uprooted and bewildered young people.

26. Too Many New Deals

A census enumerator in northern Arizona met with refusal when he asked a tribal chief if he might begin his "count of noses. . . ." A tribal council was at last called and it was agreed to let the census worker go ahead. He later learned that the Indians withheld permission until they made sure his car did not have a "John Colly license"—that is, a U. S. Department of Interior license indicating the auto belonged to the Indian agency, which is headed by John Collier. The Indians were against being included in the census if he had anything to do with it.

— *Prescott*, Arizona, *Evening Courier*

SO FAR as motives are concerned I am sure that John Collier does not deserve the hatred of the Navajo. One of the most extraordinary and devoted superintendents the Indian Bureau has ever known, he can be credited with many wise innovations in government policy. But in taking over the Indian Bureau in 1932, he inherited a complex problem, beyond his and, it may be, beyond any one man's grasp. The reservation stretches over 24,000 square miles of New Mexico, Arizona, Utah, and Colorado, and on this land the 50,000 Navajo are struggling to survive. Even before the Collier regime the range was in very bad condition from over-grazing. Something had to be done at once to reduce the number of stock the land was carrying. Collier reduced the herds drastically and set up various controls to save what was left of the range, and try to regain what had been destroyed. Almost 400,-000 sheep and goats were bought by the government and slaughtered under the eyes of the Navajo, and often left to lie where they had fallen.

This lesson in economy was a major shock to the psychology of the Navajo. The whole episode is arresting because of the conflict between Navajo and New Deal psychology. The range was so overstocked that even after so drastic a reduction the government still had to bring feed onto the reservation for the remaining animals. But it would have been better not to proceed so fast. What was necessary was to show the Navajo the need of reduction, and let him come round to the wisdom of it. If the government had merely stopped hauling feed it would have been better, perhaps.

What are young people to do if they cannot herd sheep and goats? The Indian Bureau says they can farm. It is hard to visualize the reservation as an agricultural region. Only up near Farmington where there is irrigation does it seem well adapted to crops. The reservation is remote and astonishing with wild and natural beauty. The red sandstone buttes give it tremendous style. It is filled with deep orange and very

subtle colors. Sometimes you even see imperial yellow
with vermilion, a truly remarkable pairing. The great
buttes and hills float on the edge of earth, pale blue
monsters. Often a hill reclines like a beast with half
its pelt torn off. The arroyos are frightfully clean and
stripped. At sunset one ray may shoot out from a
cloudbank to transform a single butte or hillock with
rose-mist, in a world elsewhere dead as slate. Or sometimes everything is rose-edged or flame-edged. The
sun at noon smites you with a fist of fire. It is a place of
very precious sights brought forth by aridity and light.
You feel forcibly that a land may be hallowed by
legends and by ideas of life and of death, to which you
yourself have no entrance, being utterly alien. When
you go through that country yearning and mysticism
are licking your hands like dogs. But I never heard of
anyone wanting to start farming there.

Through such a landscape go the Navajo on their
horses, born riders all of them. The women wear velvet
blouses, wide belts of silver, and big pleated skirts
like those worn by wives of the first army officers in
the West. The men too wear velveteen blouses, henna,
maroon, cherry, blue, orange, and the leather belts
with silver all round them, and wide hats. They often
have drooping mustaches, and there is always a
Chinese or Mongolian cast to their appearance.

The Navajo looks at things one way, we another.
His point of view is that the tribe could keep on living

as it had lived, and the problems would somehow take care of themselves. That is the short view of it. Collier takes the long view. Unless erosion is ended, there will soon be no grazing land, then there will be no flocks and herds, then the Navajo will have nothing to live on. So he plans for the future. Erosion does not impress the Navajo with its full significance. He considers it a detail the gods will take care of, if they wish the people to continue. In eight years there has been no altering of these two opposed views.

From the time he is able to walk a Navajo is following the flocks, and tephe, the sheep, is the mainstay of his life. When the tribe was released from military prison in 1868, there were only eight thousand Navajo and a few thousand sheep. The capacity of the Navajo to survive the severe winters and waterless summers of the open range is shown by their six-fold multiplication in sixty years. Their flocks grew to far over a million sheep. The Navajo were encouraged to increase by the agents, traders, and missionaries. The trader was forbidden to buy a ewe-lamb, and Christianity was often presented to them literally as the religion of the good shepherd. The goat is also vital to the Navajo. It lives on ranges too miserable to support sheep, and is the property of poor people. The tribe prefers kid meat to all other food, and so it is the customary food supply. The Navajo sells his wool, and naturally does not wish to kill his sheep. The goat bears two, sometimes three, kids a year, and goat milk is widely used by young and old, and to feed orphan lambs.

Maria Chabot went through the reservation last spring, stopping at hogan after hogan. She had been sent to find out how critical the situation was, and the New Mexico Association on Indian Affairs published her findings in a stirring pamphlet of observations and recommendations called *Urgent Navajo Problems.* The important recommendation is the third one: "It is strongly urged that every effort be made to obtain more adequate appropriations for the maintenance and development of irrigation projects on the Navajo Reservation."

And this brings us to the reason why the Navajo hate Collier. He promised them too much. In exchange for stock reduction they were to have dams and ditches and water, and jobs to keep them in money while they readjusted their tribal economy, direfully disturbed by the slaughter of sheep and goats, and while the promised land for crops was coming into existence. Collier thought Congress would stand by him, and so he likewise promised money to his lieutenant on the reservation, Mr. Fryer. Secretary Ickes thought Congress would stand by him and Collier, and so he promised aid to both Collier and Fryer. But Congress let them down. The collective thing, we the people through our representatives, that entity the Navajo cannot understand or visualize in any way, was at fault. All that the Navajo know is that Collier said he would give them certain things in exchange for their stock, that they fulfilled their promises (more or less), and he did not fulfill his. In other words, as they see it, Collier lied.

The winter of 1939 had been very severe, and the hungry Navajo felt that if the government had not slaughtered so many goats, they might have been eating them. Maria Chabot found bewilderment and resentment widespread. The stories people told her show how stock reduction had worked in practice.

Mary Jumbo's mother-in-law had five goats. She was ordered to reduce half, and she gave up three. "We were scared, everybody was bossin' us. No Washington people came to reduce, but policeman told us those were orders from Washington. He made the little people go first and reduce. The ones who had 'bout a thousand sheep didn't do a thing."

The Indian Bureau still threatens the rich Navajo, but in six years it has accomplished little in making them accept the new legislation. So the law, unfortunately, has been enforced against the helpless poor and not against the powerful rich. The rich Navajo, skeptical about the plan from the beginning, are now recalcitrant. They help their poor to a certain extent, and they incite and finance the agitators who go about the reservation increasing discontent. District supervisors arrest and jail these agitators on any convenient charge. They remain active, however. One of them, Tom Mariano, who is now in retreat, is a delegate to the Tribal Council itself.

Mike Yazzie said to Maria Chabot, "We feel sorry for the goats. An' they pay us one dollar for a goat. We cryin' for the goats for a long time."

Billy Johnson's wife had six thoroughbred milk goats that cost her nine dollars apiece. She could make a better living with them than with the equivalent in sheep. "She hung around the trading post crying— it was something pitiful. Then one day she went out and traded things for some scrub goats. She turned the scrubs over to policeman, and hid her good goats."

Lee Benally had seventy-seven sheep and goats. He was not down for reduction on the government chart. But the policeman, Loose Fat, not understanding the regulations, told him to sell his goats within a week. He sold sixty-one goats, and got sixty-one dollars for them. He bought a wagon instead of replacing with sheep. He said that a foreman at Shiprock had told him he would get a good job on the road and reservoir to be built. But he never got the job. Nothing has been more disillusioning to the Navajo than the fact that they never got these jobs they were promised or thought they were promised on the projected dams. They had counted on this source of money to make up for the slaughter of their stock.

A person of consequence in the tribe told Maria, "Goat reduction was the big mistake. Each jurisdiction was given a quota, but the big men held on, and the poorest people are the easiest people to take away from. A goat is worth a dollar, but the money doesn't mean anything to the family compared to the goat."

A northern trader, watching the government in its zeal strike at the roots of Navajo life when all it wished was to prune the branches, concluded, "They didn't find out how many goats a family needed, how many children there were. They wouldn't listen to individual cases."

It was a sweeping reform, based on theories and not enough guided by human feeling. If he had made the survey with the immediate welfare of the Navajo in mind instead of the immediate welfare of the land, Collier might have got somewhere and anyway would have done no damage when Congress failed him. His dealings with the Navajo amount to a perfect example of how not to go about it if you have it in mind to improve the lot of someone. The government did not take even the traders into its confidence. Many of these traders have had years of experience on the reservation and are close to the Indians. They speak their language, and no government official does, so far as I ever heard. The traders could be excellent intermediaries in passing on to the bewildered people some comprehension of the new day.

One trader said, "We don't know what this program is all about, what their plans are. A carload of college boys went through here to determine the carrying capacity of the range!" Another said, "We ain't consulted on matters of policy. All we're asked is, 'Where's the road to this place?'" And another, "The Service only comes to us when there's an emergency. Yet who does the Indian go to when he needs help? The trader. When he is sick, hungry, in trouble? I named fourteen children in the Roan Horse family alone. One morning they decided to send their children to school, and had to have five names in a hurry. I went in for names like Bill, without any R's in them, names they could say. I've delivered more babies than you can count, and buried more of the old folks."

Collier's program had sent cars flying all over the reservation, but only the Indian Service knew the meaning of the incessant activity. Surveys were made of physiography, population, distribution, sources of gross commercial income, noncommercial income, gross commercial consumption. Soils were classified, subdivided. Prairie dogs and kangaroo rats were studied for comparative infestation. There were agronomic surveys, estimates of crop production present and potential. Forestry surveys listed human, animal, fire, and fungi damage. The Navajo, in ignorance of what it portended, grew suspicious of the hundreds of questions asked him. He tore down the Soil Conservation Service tags about his fields and hogans. Some Navajo thought they themselves were to be reduced.

Grazing permits are now issued to each head of a family on the basis of his holdings in 1937. No new owners will be given permits, and, as I understand it, no herds can be increased beyond their 1937 size, until the range permits. If you had fifty sheep in 1937, and your allotted number was seventy-nine, you cannot increase your herd to seventy-nine. If you had one hundred and fifty sheep, however, you must reduce to your seventy-nine.

Collier's new program for land (and human) management divides the reservation into eighteen administrative districts, instead of the old familiar six. If the Navajo can be educated to its merits, the new system ought to be a better way of using the range. But at present he sees this multiplication of borders as a restriction and policing of his freedom. As Bob Martin, a hearty delegate to the tribal council, expressed it, "You can't go over district line and do any business. You can't go over there and get a woman. You can't even spit over there." Or, with more respect to the facts, Dizchenie Nez Begay, "I see grass growing one and a half miles from here, but I can't cross that line with my sheep. That line goes across Black Mountain and I see a lot of pine trees over there for a hogan, but if I go and cut them and somebody sees me, I will be put in jail." Or, as a cause of domestic bewilderment, "I livin' over on that reservation land. My wife have this section over here. In winter we over here—in summertime we go over there on top of that canyon line. They say we cannot go over there. I want to know about that. I do not understand about that."

To change the semi-nomadic Navajo into a farmer may be possible, for he is adaptable, and has to live. But today there is real poverty and suffering among one-quarter of the tribe. "We were hungry this winter," one Navajo told Miss Chabot. "We didn't have the piñon nuts; we had to sell them. Everywhere you go, in every district, hungry families. Ask them. Not many can get credit. Ask the traders. They know we can't pay. When I go home people come and beg until I have to hide. I can't feed all those people. 'Give me a little coffee,' and in the morning early, 'Give me a little bread.'"

A Navajo woman said, "We all turned around. Too many New Deals."

The grazing regulations are about as hard for us U. S. Americans to understand as are the income-tax regulations we ourselves struggle with. The great majority of the Navajo get only a few of the high points. Even the head men are at a loss. Kizie Yazzie Begay, delegate to the Tribal Council from District 5, said at the Window Rock Meeting in May 1939 (according to the interpreter):

"A policeman came over, maybe from Phoenix, and brought me a paper and book. This man said, 'The book holds the regulations and in it is contained the regulations by which you are permitted to graze livestock.' I looked at the book and can see a lot of marks but could not understand anything in it. You see I wear long hair and cannot understand English. This same person told me if I was not satisfied with the reading of this paper I had the privilege of calling in a lawyer to speak for me. After he said that I didn't say anything. There wasn't anything harsh in my mind and I never said anything. Shortly after this paper was put in my hands more policemen came up to me. They were heavily armed and looked like they intended carrying out the reading of this paper. He said in five days I should agree to go in accordance with the reading of this paper. I didn't say any more but said to myself, 'I don't know what this all means and since I don't understand it maybe it would be best not to say anything about it.' So I have just kept still about it since."

Apparently the summer months did not enlighten Kizie Yazzie further, for at the meeting in November he continued, "I went over to Crownpoint several days ago and a white man presided and was asked the question, just to what extent would the grazing permits keep us out or what harm can they do an individual, and this man said after the grazing permits are issued

to a person he has to comply with all the requirements
on that permit, and if he does not comply he will get
into trouble. So when I went home and told the women
about it they became afraid and said we cannot read
and don't know what is on that permit and are scared.
I am afraid of it myself because the women are afraid
of it and they are the ones who are afraid they will
get in trouble over it and it should be made much
clearer than it is."

Mr. Fryer is the superintendent of the reservation
and responsible for the reforms. He is an agronomist
first and last, with an excellent scientific reputation.
I am told that he and his staff are fascinated by the
problem of reclaiming the reservation. But human nature is human nature. Far from the comfortable and
expensive government buildings at Window Rock on
the edge of the reservation, a Navajo told Miss Chabot
that a former supervisor, the kind of man Indians trust
and go to for help, had once taken a group of them into
his confidence. He had said, "Well, boys, we want to
try to do something. I don't know if we can, but we
can try." That is the kind of talk a Navajo likes, without promises. "But," said the Indian, "we see airplane
fly over—a car go by sixty miles an hour—that's Mr.
Fryer."

It is no bare-faced cynicism on the part of the bureau when it tells the young people to farm. Strange
as it may appear, the bureau really means it. The offi-

cials are still thinking in terms of the dams and irrigation ditches they promised the Navajo. But there is now no money for them. Congress balked at the expense. There is little money for the reservation, for any purpose. The Navajo has always done a little farming. He has put in corn where he knew the ground contained hidden moisture, as do the Hopi. When you fly over the Hopi towns you wonder why their little fields take such extraordinary shapes. The reason is that through the centuries the Hopi have learned how far the moisture beneath the surface will suffice for a crop. They plant the corn a foot deep with their sticks, and know to within less than a foot where to leave off planting.

Recently some Navajo children have died of malnutrition. The Navajo believe rightly or wrongly that the lack of goat's milk makes them liable to tuberculosis. But they have survived so much already in their long history that we can hope they will survive the improvements of Mr. Collier and Mr. Fryer, and the indifference of Congress. If Congress appropriates enough money to keep the work going on the irrigation projects, the Navajo will win in time. If Congress fails to do so the results, I am afraid, will be tragic.

27. Sand-Paintings

The Museum of Navajo Ceremonial Art cordially invites you
to attend a private showing of the Navajo Mountain Chant
film, at the Laboratory of Anthropology, Old Pecos Road,
Santa Fe, on Thursday afternoon, November 14, at four
o'clock. . . .
                            —MARY C. WHEELWRIGHT, Director

ALICE CORBIN HENDERSON, who sent us the invita-
tion, and who is Curator of the Museum, wrote
underneath it, "Don't miss this—it is very beautiful
and unusual." I would not have missed it for worlds.
The film showed more of concealed Navajo life than
an outsider like myself would see by a hundred trips
to the reservation. Its authors were Lorenzo Hubbell,
a man the Navajo have known for years and whom
they trust completely, and Mrs. Laura Adams Armer
of California, a student of Navajo life. It is a documentary film, and pictures a man who had fallen sick
of a mental trouble (the Navajo seem to have almost
as many mental troubles as U. S. Americans do), and
the intricate procedures called into play to cure him.

If you are troubled by dreaming of a rattlesnake,
or if like the man in this film you keep dreaming of

your dead children, or if your trouble is a literal one like not being able to hold anything on your stomach, you try to induce a medicine man to propitiate the god or gods you must somehow have offended. Even if you are not a Navajo but a Hopi or a white, he may be inclined to help you. The ceremony may begin with four days of preparation, then pass to nine days for sand-paintings, and end with four days of readjustment to the world.

Each painting is destroyed before sunset on the day it is made, for it has served its purpose. During the four subsequent days that adjust him to the world again, the patient, so I hear, has to be careful about certain matters which differ in the individual case, and which the medicine man warns him about—perhaps he must not sleep in the daytime, or perhaps he must avoid work that deals with fire and water. He must always be careful not to touch or be with people who have never had the sing. Its benefits, I infer, are designed to be permanent. In the course of his purification, the gods have imparted power to him which will not leave him, yet which, in the casual and irresponsible ways of contact, might well injure people less fortunate.

The whole affair is attended by the most scrupulous attention to detail. Everyone agrees that it is so, and the obvious reason is that the deities appealed to descend to inspect each painting. If each is not absolutely shipshape, they are offended and withdraw, and if they withdraw there is no cure for the patient. But if all is right in the pictured harmony of forces, the spirits are pleased, and remain. With the patient seated in the midst of the painting, the chanter, or shaman, or medicine man begs the spirits concerned to forgive him for whatever evil he has done and to help him out of his trouble. Then with his eagle plume the shaman carries the touch of the pictured deity to the living mortal, beginning with his feet, and so on up his body. As he does this he wipes out the corresponding portions of the picture. These actions suffice to drive the devils out of the patient's mouth.

The body of the patient, being itself painted, becomes a living part of the painting. He may have the sun on his chest, the moon on his back, lightnings over his shoulders, snakes in his insteps. When the patient's devils are all gone out of him, the shaman gathers up the sand of the painting and takes it to the east but pours it out to the north. When you take away the imaged gods who have afflicted the patient, you take away the cause of the illness. It is clear, and it is finished.

The shaman is trained for years in the work of picturing in a way that will give the onlooker some idea of them, the great contraries which by their varying tension preserve the balance of things. When he seats the patient on the sand-painting he bases him on an image of harmonious opposites. When he draws the symbolic colors and shapes on up from the sand to the living limbs, he paints him into the universe, adjusts him to the play of many-sided forces. To the imagination, religion could hardly make graphic a more colossal medicine. The patient both as individual and as genus melts into meaning. Meaning ascends from the earth to all his parts. Most of all it ascends to what in a man gives unity to those parts, call it heart, soul, mind, or spirit; and so it banishes, figuratively at least, the maladjustment that prevents singleness of purpose.

The medicine man may use fifteen different plants for one painting, many of them pungent. He may gather most of them near the hogan, red pentstemon, for example, spearmint, chokecherry, and scrub oak. Or he may travel a considerable distance to secure them. The patient will hire two helpers to chop these medicines fine. For four days before and after, everyone connected with the sing is continent. The four days beforehand are devoted to cleansing and to preparing sacrifices to the various gods. The design of the painting often stays about the same the first four days. The intricacy of the rituals and the number of details to be prepared keep the medicine man busy from before dawn to nearly midnight. There are details that only the medicine man knows, others that only the patient and helpers share with him.

Apparently only chanter and helpers (never women)
see a sand-painting at its most beautiful, for the last
touches upon it begin to obscure it. And when the patient comes he has first of all to sprinkle cornmeal
over each figure, under the chanter's directions. Sand-
painting patterns transferred to blankets and rugs, or
to the walls of railway hotels, can be remarkably ugly.
But those who know say that the originals are never
ugly, they have such grace of proportion. The different sizes of the woven pieces cause elongation, or the
figures become squat through compression. It is such
a distortion as you might see of yourself, for example,
in passing the highly polished curve of a Pullman cor-
ridor.

Medicine men no doubt find it impossible to convey symbolic meanings to whites who lack all background for them except perhaps the reading of Navajo
myths in scholarly renderings. Thus it is impossible to
know whether every sand-painting is intended to repeat a myth or not. Perhaps many of them suggest
snatches of myth, or even nuances of their symbolic
meanings, chosen for definite reasons. But sand-paintings are invariably studies in symmetry and balance.
Two is against two, four against four. Everything has
its opposite, counterpart, vis-a-vis. Three sides of the
painting a rainbow frames. The open side is always
to the rising sun, and this gateway of the sun is care-

fully guarded by pictured deities. The paintings vary in size from two inches to the great representations of the night and mountain chants, often twelve feet in diameter. The meanings may also vary between the esoteric and the forms of equivalence an ordinary person might understand. For example, the band of yellow corn pollen from mouth to mouth may represent "one word," that is, each figure says the same word, and it signifies agreement, accord. The hands and feet, of corn pollen and crossed, may well mean friendship and love. There may be such axiomatic figures that the student of sand-paintings would soon learn.

Alice Corbin Henderson told me once about being out on the reservation; she was very tired and dreaded the cold and the staying-up all night to see a Navajo ceremonial. She and Miss Wheelwright watched a sand-painting being made. Soon she felt perfectly well, and noticed it suddenly.

The Museum of Navajo Ceremonial Art in Santa Fe is the only museum from which I ever emerge refreshed. I attribute it to the effect of the designs of the sand-paintings copied on the walls. These works of religious art contain depths and qualities which those who are qualified to do so should study and tell us about. Sand-paintings are supreme and extraordinary expressions of psychology. Their purpose, I suppose, if it can be phrased in colloquial terms, is to make patient, participants, and onlookers feel "all right." You cannot really and truly feel all right unless you have a harmony in yourself like the harmony of nature round you. For this reason the medicine bundle contains symbols of all universal forces, the shaman tries to bring them all into play, with his scrupulous technique is forever seeking the perfect touch. A people is fortunate whose gods lay upon it the necessity of tending to all the opposites, so as not to become spiritually lopsided or dismembered. But the rituals are cumbersome for an age in which even religion grows more and more streamlined.

The lame old shaman in the Hubbell film had one of the wisest and gentlest faces I have ever seen. I often think about the old men in the southwest country who lead consecrated lives. They may or may not be actively toiling and preaching with words for a better world. It is more likely that their activity is intense and circumscribed. They are observing in the careful ways that lead to praise, the handiwork of the creator. They do not regard his handiwork as culminating in themselves or in mankind, do not regard mankind notably or out of proportion at all, but rather they direct their meditation to the beauty, the strangeness, and the mystery of the world. Those old men—they may be bearded Mormon elders, or Catholic or Protestant priests, or Navajo shamans, or Pueblo caciques,

I would not know who they all are—but it seems to me I can feel their presence in the spiritual stability of the region, and I believe they are laying at God's feet a life of subtle and private worship past our general comprehension.

28. Schlatter

With every day of his stay in Albuquerque Francis Schlader, the "Healer," "El Gran Hombre," or whatever else he may be called, is making friends and converts. Probably no man who has put forward a startling proposition in modern times has been more thoroughly doubted than Schlader. . . . Men who a week ago would have driven him from the community as a fraud and an impostor are today among his staunchest friends and supporters.

—*The Albuquerque Democrat,* July 27, 1895

HEALERS seem to me extremely important people. As to the mystery of their being able to heal, I do not understand it at all but am willing to take much of it for granted. There is a well-known and much-discussed footnote on page 148 of *Man, the Unknown,* in which, speaking of what goes on at Lourdes, Dr. Carrel calls miraculous cures "stubborn irreducible facts" that bear witness to organic and mental processes of which we know nothing. It is not the ability of healers to heal that occupies me but rather the fact that they *care* to heal. In the persons of Núñez and this man Schlatter we see human nature unbelievably sensitized to the curable suffering of others.

Three and a half centuries after Núñez this Francis Schlatter, an Alsatian, appeared in Arizona, Colorado, and New Mexico enduring great privations and healing people. The 1893-94 strikes in Denver and general starvation and illness among the poor had "deranged" him, as various people including the clergy said. The suffering about him caused such suffering within him that he no longer cared for anything but to be "as close to the Father" as possible. He understood the Father to say he should walk the railroads and be of help, as a way of preparing himself for the reception of power. Unlike Núñez, he had to struggle a long time to receive it.

The routes Schlatter followed during the next few years form a great cross on the map. The horizontal bar of this cross runs from the West coast to Topeka, the vertical bar from Denver south into Old Mexico, and the center of the transit itself is about at Santa Fe, though he never visited that town so far as I know.

Like Núñez, Schlatter wrote an account of these journeys. It is abbreviated and even incoherent, but as with lightning flashes reveals a good deal about people. One night he was sleeping under a sheet he had pegged down near the tracks. The section boss came by and said:

"Aren't you afraid of rattlesnakes? The country is full of them."

"I? No. I have no need to be afraid."

"Then he asked me many questions," Schlatter continues. "I told him what my mission was, and he believed." In another place two officers of the law came to arrest him. He told them he was preparing himself to heal, and they said, "We had better leave you alone," and went off quietly. Another time, on a dirt road paralleling the tracks, a man came by driving a bay team. The man questioned him.

"I know you boys from Denver have it very hard. I have to ask you all these questions because I am sheriff of this county. Where are you going?"

"To Hot Springs."

"You have a terrible walk ahead of you. Have you any more hope?"

"More than ever." The remark puzzled the sheriff as he drove on.

He stopped at houses for food when the Father permitted it. Sometimes people were good to him, sometimes they were not. The railroad workers always were. At one house a man asked him what he was doing, and Schlatter explained. "That is a novelty in America," said the man. Another man said, "You have a hard way to serve the Lord." A woman who had fed him well, said, "Oh, I read those things, but I don't believe them any more." A well-dressed young woman pointed to his unkempt figure in a village street and said to her companions, "What do you call that thing?" It stung him to the quick. An Irish section boss had him sit down with him for supper in the section-house and asked him the usual questions. When Schlatter had answered, the boss said, "You know your business. I know mine. I never criticize anyone. What they tell me I believe." They had a "happy" evening together, Schlatter says, and the boss gave him a pair of overalls.

These tramps across country opened Schlatter's eyes. "As the magnitude of the work necessary to be done was being unfolded to me gradually, I said to Father: 'I have not will power enough for such a terrible work such as you tell me I must do.' And Father said: 'No, not now, but you will have pretty soon.'"

Within the next two months, he says he felt his will power grow, and his indignation against legalized robbery strengthen. Robbed himself in the Mojave desert of his little money and less food, he says, "These two men are not the only robbers on this earth. Who made the laws and then betrayed the trust which the nation gave; turned and robbed the masses for the benefit of the few?"

The crossing of the desert without food or water was one of Schlatter's considerable feats. Another, as hard to believe, was his crossing over Bill Williams Mountain in the dead of winter. "Father insisted on it." He herded sheep among the piñones near Williams for a time, and spent five days alone with a Navajo medicine man, Ho-ka-ni-ridge as he spells it. Proceed-

ing through Winslow and Gallup he reached Albuquerque. There he stayed with people who believed
in him, in Old Town. He had already begun a forty-
day fast, and here he first undertook seriously the
work of healing. He attracted crowds, and the newspapers wrote him up. Among the native people, who
called him "El Sanador," he seems to have made a
few sure cures, and he was markedly successful in
alleviating pain.

Schlatter left Albuquerque for Denver August 21,
1895. When the papers said he was going to Denver
"for public work," thousands came to the way sta-
tions for his blessing, and stood on the tracks to prevent the train from going until they received it. Schlatter became the guest of a Mr. Fox who lived in North
Denver. He had healed Mrs. Fox in Old Town, and
Mr. Fox had sent him the railroad ticket. An alley ran
behind the Fox yard, and the healer took up his position there behind the fence every morning at nine
o'clock. Long before then the line was formed, and
this line was kept in order by willing followers. At
noon he took a recess of one hour, and he tried to close
his public work daily at four o'clock. Many persons
retained their positions in line all night, to be sure of
treatment the following day. Joseph Wolff, in his account, says that to see the crowd you would think all
the world was sick. As many as eighty thousand persons touched his hand or were touched and blessed

by him, and he appears to have made many cures. The last day alone he treated over five thousand. He took each sufferer's hand into his warm clasp and said an almost inaudible prayer. Often he was heard to say, "Not I, but the Father. Believe in the Father." A Negro woman tried to give him a fifty-cent piece. When he let her go she shouted, "Glory be to God, I'se healed and I'se got my fifty cents!"

During his months in Denver it was never heard that he accepted as much as a cent for his ministrations. The Denver papers reported even more respectfully on his doings than the Albuquerque press had done. One paper said, "The scene was most impressive, full of dignity and sincerity. Schlatter impressed many as looking like Jesus with his light hair curling down on his shoulders, his fine face and exalted expression. He seemed to be simple-minded, fairly intelligent, and above all sincere." Even in cold weather he dressed as in Albuquerque, in well-washed blue jeans and shirt, and strapped sandals on his bare feet.

The morning of November 14, 1895, the Fox household found the healer's room vacant and a note on the pillow saying, "Mr. Fox.—My mission is finished. Father takes me away. Good-bye.—Francis Schlatter." The disappointment of the waiting crowd is what most causes you to reflect in the whole story. People who were there said it was like taking light and hope out of life and leaving only desolation, only the industrial age. Many wept uncontrollably, others cursed and swore, most of them moved through the alley and round the square with leaden feet. They reduced the fence to splinters for mementoes, and even scooped up the earth where Schlatter had stood. In his bedroom were found countless unanswered letters, many containing handkerchiefs for his blessing. The amount of mail he received was without parallel, and he had devoted every moment possible to keeping pace with it. Wolff claims it is doubtful if even a presidential candidate up to then had ever received so many letters in the same length of time.

You would suspect exhaustion as the reason for his departure, but he was not unduly fatigued by his weeks of uninterrupted concentration. I have rather heard it said that he was to be summoned as a witness against persons charged with using the mails to defraud by selling handkerchiefs he had blessed. If this is true, it is sufficiently ironic. His reason for never accepting money for treatments was his belief that greed causes nearly all crimes against humanity.

But if he had no money, he had a white horse, a saddle and bridle, and saddlebags, for Mr. Fox had presented them to him. Reporters and detectives were immediately on his trail, and the papers warned every hamlet to be on the watch. Fortunately, Schlatter escaped this net of unwarranted activity. The next day one of those early blizzards that Colorado dreads visited the serrated mountains south of Denver. People were lost and frozen to death at Palmer Lake, and everyone accepted the healer's death as a certainty. Nonetheless, seven weeks and six days later, in January, 1896, astride his white horse, Schlatter stopped at the Morley ranch, in southwestern New Mexico. People who know the country consider this his greatest physical exploit, for Putney Mesa is badly broken terrain, with no marked trails; no old-timer would attempt it in such weather, hardly even a Navajo.

Since her husband's death, Mrs. Ada Morley of Hermosillo Ranch, Datil, had managed big cattle ranches and brought up her children in a tradition of learning, courage, and good citizenship. It had at first seemed impossible to arrange it, but she had been able that autumn through a stroke of good luck to send her son Ray to Ann Arbor, and her daughter Agnes to Stanford. Thus Mrs. Morley was alone in her large ranch house twenty miles from the nearest neighbor. She reports that she was sitting by the fire reading Henry Wood's *Ideal Suggestion,* and had just read, "I am soul, I am free; pain is friendly. God is here," when the door opened. It was her dour and secretive cowboy, Billy Swingle.

"They's a tramp," he announced, "a-layin' out by the barn and he's took down the fence and let his horse at the haystack."

"He'll freeze to death," said Mrs. Morley. "Invite him to come in."

When Schlatter entered the doorway Mrs. Morley at once recognized him as the Denver healer. She said later, "I saw a vast and happier future, and knew I was free."

Schlatter stayed at the Datil ranch until early April. By then people were beginning to know where he was. His washwoman bottled the soapy water and sold it as a cure-all. He remarked, "Father said I must go as soon as people learn I am here. They have been talking it quietly for a long time."

When he parted from Mrs. Morley he asked her to repeat the Lord's Prayer as he himself said it: "Thy will *will* be done." Evidence was found much later of his death in Old Mexico, where he had apparently continued his ministration, in small villages.

29. The Gallup Riot

This little mining town, often racked and torn by labor dis-
putes and bloody warfare, again today was an armed village. . . . Yesterday's riot left Sheriff Carmichael and a miner
named Velarde dead, and seven persons wounded. . . .

> —*Santa Fe New Mexican*, April
> 4, 1935. (Dispatch from Gallup)

STRIKES are among the absorbing events that happen in a nation on the way to becoming a
democracy. Many a strike bares every important nerve
and sinew of the body politic, and shows it in relation
to all the others.

Gallup is one of the six or seven largest towns in
New Mexico, a place of 8,000 people; in addition to
having coal mines, it is a division point on the railway
and a distributing center for the Navajo reservation.
The Gallup American Coal Company, a subsidiary of
important eastern copper interests, permitted the
miners who worked their Gamerco mine to settle on
an undesirable tract of its land just outside the city.
This tract was known as Chihuahuita, or little Chihuahua; many of the miners were unnaturalized Mex-

icans imported from the vicinity of that Mexican city. The company leased each man his lot for a nominal rent but subject to eviction without notice. Few of the miners knew English, and none seems to have understood the significance of the eviction clause. Simple people, they thought they were safe on the land, and in the two- or three-room adobe houses they built on it, often with their own hands.

In the spring of 1935 it became known that the coal company no longer owned Chihuahuita. What it had in mind in allowing Chihuahuita to pass out of its control is not of record. State Senator Clarence Vogel had acquired title to it. What he had in mind by buying these barren little hills, and what he paid for them, is not of record, either. The winter before as a member of the state legislature, Vogel had opposed a bill, which was defeated, to prevent evictions during the period of involuntary unemployment.

None of the five local coal companies was doing well. Oil and gas had largely replaced coal for heating and hundreds of miners were out of work; even the unnaturalized Mexicans had joined a local of the National Miners' Union. They, too, struck in 1933 for better working conditions and for the right to organize as guaranteed under the National Recovery Act. Gallup submitted to martial law for five months, with many men including mine guards deputized, and a company of the National Guard at hand by order of the Governor. The police apprehended a number of labor leaders and confined them in a stockade at the fair grounds. The settlement negotiated by Major Moore, the government mediator, in January, 1934, was a technical victory for the miners, since they won eight of their eleven demands. But the mine owners, with the low level of employment, found it impossible to reemploy miners who had been active in the strike. The miners thus lost confidence in government help, and a number of them had become Communists. A radical organizer said there were no Communists in Gallup before the strike, but afterward about one hundred and fifty.

Gallup business suffered from the long strike. The members of the National Guard were furious at the waste of their time, and New Mexico taxpayers had to pay $90,000 for their keep while on duty—a bill that might well have gone to the mine owners. During this period, as before and after so far as I have ever heard, the distant owners showed no sign of being sorry, or even of being aware, that they had handed Gallup an extremely difficult social problem.

It is impossible not to sympathize with Gallup in the predicament it was in. It is still a town in process of being born, still part of the Old West with the Navajo and the cowboys, yet pierced daily by the streamlined aluminum trains and the swift cars of the transcontinental highway. Unable to unite its former stages with the industrial age, it finds baffling the simplest group-problems. It lies sprawled out on its bare hills at the mercy of the southwest sun, unsightly as the worst of the Pennsylvania mining towns. Other semi-arid towns, smaller in size and worse situated, have planted shade trees and kept them watered. The Gallup churches appear to have no leadership in civic affairs, nor do the liberal professions lend the place dignity. There has been no banding together of citizens for humane purposes, yet even in money nothing costs a town more than its inhumanity. But Gallup is one of the few industrial cities in the Southwest. Her problems are not those of her more fortunate sister cities, Santa Fe, Roswell, Albuquerque, Prescott, Phoenix, and so she faces her future by herself.

Her problems are not insoluble, however, and in another direction something is happening. Gallup holds an intertribal Indian ceremonial each August, which attracts hundreds of tourists. Somebody in Gallup or near there, perhaps an Indian trader, originated and worked out the details of this idea, a lucrative one and free of eastern corporations. It could not be as successful as it is without the co-operation of the rank and file of the citizenry. Because it teaches people to work together for their common good, and involves their being hosts to other people, the Indian ceremonial contains within itself the key to a better future for Gallup.

As owner of Chihuahuita, Senator Vogel brought suit in court against one Victor Campos, a Mexican living in the United States illegally. A constable with an order for possession moved out Campos's furniture and nailed up the door of his house. This action frightened everyone who lived on Vogel's land; if such a fate happened to Campos it could happen to all of them. In Chihuahuita three hundred people lived in seventy-five or more houses.

When he came home, Campos broke open his flimsy door and put his furniture back inside. He was helped by Exiquio Navarro, a short swarthy Mexican known to the police as an active union man, and by a fiery old woman named Mrs. Lovato. All three were at once arrested. Mrs. Lovato was released, but the two men were taken before William J. Bickel, justice of the peace.

The next Sunday afternoon the unemployed miners held a meeting in Spanish American Hall. Its primary purpose was to appoint a committee to ask for more adequate relief. The chairman, Juan Ochoa, tended to this business at once. Ochoa is a slim quiet intelligent man, a United States citizen born in Mexico, equally at home in English or Spanish. Then, with the eviction of Campos fresh in mind, and his illegal detention with Navarro bringing up former times of terror, the unemployed miners voted to send a committee to the sheriff, to ask whether they could provide bail and counsel for the two prisoners. Ochoa appointed such a committee. He conducted an orderly meeting; there was oratory but no incendiary remarks, and the police did not interfere.

The miners' committee went to the sheriff at once. Carmichael declined to let them see the prisoners, but he told them Justice Bickel would hear the case next morning at nine o'clock. In Chihuahuita the news caused a good deal of talk. A fat cross-eyed Mexican named Leandro Velarde, who is something of a clown, was reported later as saying that he had a grudge against Sheriff Carmichael, and the sheriff against him; that he had a big belly and was ready to stick it out for the poor; and that "the officers could get their guns if they wanted to; all the miners needed was toothpicks." Later in court the prosecution attempted without success to prove that *pica diente* meant ice pick, or the pick you dig coal with; and Leandro's joke, turning sour, runs through the entire record.

Monday morning the sheriff took his prisoners to court under guard of three armed deputies. Coal Avenue was quiet, but during the next half hour while Bickel was hearing the case of a Navajo, a crowd of somewhere between fifty and two hundred and fifty men, women, and children gathered on the street outside the justice's office. Two federal officers with the Navajo in tow left the office and passed through this crowd without difficulty. The justice admitted no one from the street, though the trial was public. Present were only State Senator Vogel, his attorney, the defendants, and police officers.

Navarro asked for time to procure counsel. Bickel granted the request and postponed the case until Tuesday. Sheriff Carmichael decided to take the prisoners out the back way. To hide the maneuver he stationed four police officers inside Bickel's plateglass window on Coal Avenue. The crowd, mystified and unable to see, pressed forward and broke the window. Someone yelled, "They're taking them out by the alley," and the crowd surged up Coal Avenue and round the corner into Third Street. The alley leads from Third Street to Second, where the jail stands, and Bickel's office opens on it.

Fred Montoya, former mine guard and deputy, testified later that when he opened Bickel's door the crowd was coming down the alley with Leandro and Ignacio Velarde in the forefront, and that Leandro shook his fist and called him "desgraciado" (which means literally only "disgraced" but is a fighting word). Montoya retired from the door, and someone else looked out and saw Solomón Esquivel reaching inside his coat as though for a weapon. It was also testified that Solomón yelled, "You move back! Leave them to us!"

Sheriff Carmichael and Dee Roberts, the first deputy, stepped out into the alley with Navarro between them. The other two deputies, Hoy Boggess and

"Bobcat" Wilson, followed with Campos. Dee Roberts testified that he saw Juan Ochoa threatening him with a claw hammer. Hoy Boggess saw someone grab for his prisoner, and he hurled a tear-gas bomb into the rushing crowd. Boggess was then knocked down. A shot was fired and, according to Roberts' account of it, by Ignacio Velarde, standing across the alley. Roberts saw Carmichael turn at the sound with blood coming from his face. He lowered the sheriff to the pavement, drew his gun, and shot Ignacio. He also shot Solomón Esquivel. Solomón fell, but he started to get up, and Roberts shot him again. On the stand Roberts swore that four or five miners were kicking and beating the prostrate Hoy Boggess, among them Ochoa and one Manuel Avitia. Boggess struggled to his feet, and just then Bobcat cried out, "I'm shot!" Boggess grabbed Bobcat's gun, and he and Roberts fired at the fast retreating crowd. The tear gas was blinding everybody, but twelve or fifteen shots rang out. Two were wounded in the crowd, one a woman.

A mine guard standing in Coal Avenue said he saw Manuel Avitia run out of the alley with a pistol. Chief of Police Kelcey Presly also saw Avitia with something "that looked like a gun," but when arrested he was unarmed. The guns said to be in the possession of the two miners whom Dee Roberts killed, Ignacio Velarde and Solomón Esquivel, were never found. Sheriff Carmichael's own gun had not been fired. He had been shot twice; either shot might have proved fatal, and he died instantly. One of the bullets lodged in his left shoulder and was recovered. The bullet that wounded Bobcat Wilson was also recovered.

Dee Roberts was now sheriff. He and his bigger brother Bob had for years taken turns being sheriff of McKinley County. At this time by some political chance Carmichael occupied the office, with the brothers as his deputies. Dee Roberts swore out John Doe warrants, deputized dozens of citizens, and went out to Chihuahuita to seek the missing guns. They failed to find them, but they came back with union and communist literature, and evidence that various miners were unnaturalized, which was of course no secret in Gallup. Roberts arrested more than a hundred people, and crowded them into the city and county jails. Sixteen women and four children spent a stifling night in two small cells. Prisoners for whom there was no room in the jails were guarded in the courtrooms.

A riot and the murder of a sheriff is sober news, and the effect of it on those who read the papers, as always in such matters, was as automatic as when you strike high C on your piano and your dog howls. Gallup was a high C for the different mentalities that compose society. Among social reactions some are standard. You can be sure that certain groups will see the situation as a chance to press their own purposes, whether to drive troublesome aliens out of town, or to push revolution-

ary ideas for remodeling society. You can count also
on the reaction of conservative people. Reading of the
seizure of communist literature, they will regard the
whole affair as an outbreak of the "class war." And as
class war it will be viewed by radicals. People aware of
the importance to democracy of full respect for civil
rights, will react to the invasion of such rights. You can
count on that, too. People with a chronic sympathy for
the underdog will fly off the handle when they hear
that miners who do not understand English have been
arrested and held without counsel. Another kind of
person always shows up, unpredictable as the weather,
full of zeal whether for national institutions or rights
of capital or rights of labor, and capable of going to
any extreme. These latter are apt to be people full of
suppressed fury from private troubles, who seek relief
by partisanship in dispute.

And so the stage was set and the curtain rose.

The American Civil Liberties Union sent A. L.
Wirin from Los Angeles to Gallup to see to it that the
miners received justice. Mr. Wirin, a tall athletic young
man, was aggressive and an outsider—two points that
found no favor with Gallup citizens or police. Someone told him to be on his way, and he boarded a train
for Santa Fe to seek support. He found it, for the capital city contained persons quick to sympathize with
the miners. Fifteen of them organized a New Mexico
Branch of the Civil Liberties Union, as a Gallup de-

fense committee. They retained Wheaton Augur, a Santa Fe attorney, to co-operate with Mr. Wirin. Clarence Lynch of the International Labor Defense also joined the defense counsel.

In Gallup armed men were posted at every corner, for the grapevine telegraph was active. Wheaton Augur and Ann Webster drove there from Santa Fe on business for the Gallup defense committee. They found fire hose stretched out on the street, and on inquiry learned that "a bunch of Santa Fe lawyers were coming down to start a mass meeting." Mrs. Webster had been a lawyer in Washington before she came to Santa Fe. She and Augur, slender and fragile people, kept silent, greatly surprised that rumors of their approach had entangled a rumored mass meeting with reprisal by fire hose.

Gallup lay in the jurisdiction of Judge Miguel A. Otero, Jr., a consistent liberal, and the most notable contemporary member of a famous family. He is short and fair and boyish, though with a shiny pate, is well schooled, and remains unruffled by extravagances from either side in a dispute. In Gallup, Carl Howe, a communist organizer but not a lawyer, had appeared for the miners and waived preliminary hearing. Mr. Wirin and Mr. Lynch, in Santa Fe, demanded one. Judge Otero granted it without demur, and ordered the defendants brought to Santa Fe and lodged in the penitentiary. In Gallup the number of those held had by

now been reduced, first from one hundred and fifty to
fifty-two, and then from fifty-two to forty-five. Most of
them spoke no English, and they marched into Otero's
courtroom with folded arms like convicts, ragged and
bewildered. One, Bill Cutin, was a Negro, and one a
Slav who spoke neither Spanish nor English. It was
ruled that the proceedings should not concern the
Slav.

The crowd that filled the courtroom that morning
contained both old-timers and newcomers. Judge
Otero invited the members of the defense committee
to sit inside the rail. As a concession to conservatives,
he stationed a policeman at the door to frisk all
comers. Dee Roberts was on the stand a long while.
You rarely have a chance to see a man like the sheriff
of McKinley County, and I looked at him with interest.
He was middle-aged, clean-shaven, and had no extra
flesh. In a county like McKinley the sheriff would find
the industrial age only one of his woes. He had to
handle the woes of the frontier and of the pre-frontier
ages also, with the Navajo reservation at hand, the bad
Navajo and the bad whites, horse-rustlers and bootleggers. He had the vital uncontrollable town to look
after, with its gamblers and women and saloons, the
tremendous Saturday nights, the aborigines, cowboys,
old-timers, characters as fantastic as Paul Bunyan. Dee
Roberts seemed alert and uneasy. As law-enforcement

officer he had to be ready to duck, dodge, swing, or shoot at any moment.

Yet the West has a tradition of men who have enforced the law in difficult localities and over long periods of time without killing anybody. William Martin is such an officer. "Uncle Billy" Tilghman who fought for the law fifty years, first in Dodge City, then in Oklahoma, killed rarely, only when he had to, and always gave the other man time to draw. It is true that his generosity cost him his life, in old age; but it made him an impressive figure in the state, and at his death he lay in state in the capitol, and governors and senators paid him their respects.

The miners were stocky, uncouth, and ignorant, but elemental and unkillable like the piñones and sabinas of the country. At least they seemed unkillable compared to the Americans in the courtroom, and made the latter appear a tense and nerve-worn race. But I remembered too what a friend had told me, after visiting Chihuahuita, that they were not all of them tough and sturdy. She had seen a miner's wife, tall, slender, beautiful with the beauty of the famous painting of Beatrice Cenci; and she had seen ailing children. The people were so afraid of being arrested, she said, that they literally fled at the approach of Americans. She saw children sucking halves of oranges, and hoping someone might be helping the miners, she asked where they got them. The children pointed to a city dump.

The third day David Levinson arrived from Philadelphia to represent the International Labor Defense Association. He was a small, keen-faced man who wore formal morning clothes and a pince-nez on a long black ribbon. I remember that he demanded the withdrawal of the word "nigger," which he thought he had heard when one of the state's attorneys with a southern drawl had said "Negra." Bill Cutin, the colored gentleman concerned, grinned delightedly when the judge rebuked Levinson and told him to prick up his ears.

Justice of the Peace Bickel was placed on the stand, but he contradicted himself under cross-examination and the judge declared his testimony invalid. His Honor ruled out the testimony of one of the key witnesses also, when it was shown that a miner whom he had positively identified as being at the scene of the shooting, was working in the mine at the time. District Attorney Chavez asked the dismissal of three more defendants. His Honor granted the request, and the strategy of the prosecution bared itself when the three men were at once rearrested by immigration officers for being in the country illegally. Mr. Levinson's suavity vanished and he snatched an officer's arm. There were cries of "He's interfering with a federal officer," but Judge Otero had swiftly left the courtroom. Nothing came of this incident except that the defense charged the state with getting rid of several important alibi witnesses, and sent telegrams of protest to Secretary Perkins in Washington.

When the evidence was in, Mr. Wirin made a heated plea to allow the miners to return "to their miserable shacks, their back-breaking work in the coal mines, to relief or starvation or whatever their lot in life." Augur also spoke, contending that the evidence indicated no intent to do harm, and that the Gallup officers were prejudiced and panicky. But testimony had tended to show that ten of the miners had been in the crowd in the alley, four of them armed. Under New Mexico law, as well as the law invoked in the Haymarket case and upheld by the Supreme Court in Washington, all the members of a mob may be held as participants in a murder. His Honor held ten men for the murder of the sheriff and for aiding a prisoner to escape. The four who were armed he held without bail—Juan Ochoa, whom Dee Roberts said he saw flourishing a claw hammer, Avitia, whom someone had seen with a gun in his hand, Leandro Velarde, he of the toothpick or ice pick, and one Augustin Calvillo, whom Chief Presly had disarmed of a club. The other six the Judge held in seventy-five dollars bail, and the rest of the party he sent back to Gallup in a state 'bus.

This decision satisfied neither side. Judge Otero was no longer saluted in the radical press as a Daniel come to judgment, and conservatives felt they had been betrayed by a member of their own class. Fear increased

on both sides. David Levinson, wishing to go to Gallup
to gather evidence, demanded police protection, and
Judge Otero designated Earl Irish, a state trooper, to
accompany him. With them also went Robert Minor,
who had come on as representative of the *Daily
Worker*, and two Santa Feans, Katharine Gay, formerly a newspaperwoman in New York, to report the
case for *The Nation*, and Ted Stevenson, a novelist, to
report it for *The New Masses*.

In Gallup the committee found El Navaho, the Harvey hotel, full of people whom they described as
"stooges, rats, and spies." Stevenson wrote, "This is a
town of concealed weapons." Katharine Gay described
the terror the party felt "in that debased little mining
town, their every move followed, constantly under the
eyes of ignorant, Faulkner-like men." Afraid of dicto-
graphs in their rooms, they met in the lobby to discuss
possible witnesses with Mrs. Bartol, the miners' representative. Even there they thought they were eaves-
dropped upon by passing gunmen. And so Levinson
and Minor went outside and sat in a car with Mrs.
Bartol.

In a few moments other cars drew up alongside
them, according to Mrs. Bartol, and masked men got
out and shoved guns into their ribs. She said she saw
Levinson and Minor struck on the head, dragged into
another car, and thrown on the floor. She heard Minor
call for help, but though El Navaho is in the center of

the town, no one responded. Mrs. Bartol watched the cars cross the tracks and start north. She started to follow, but "a masked youth" near-by, according to her story, suggested that she mind her own business. She ran into the hotel crying, "They've got them!"

The defense committee got on the long-distance phone at once, calling the governor, the attorney general, Judge Otero, the United States attorney, and the *Albuquerque Journal*. Two hours later, at eleven o'clock, Dee Roberts, the sheriff, arrived. At three in the morning Governor Tingley, his slumbers troubled by the repeated telephoning, agreed to send additional troopers. At noon the next day Mr. Levinson called the Governor from the Indian hospital at Tohatchi, twenty-five miles from Gallup. He demanded police and military protection, and an investigation of the kidnapping. He and Minor were safe, he said, but shaken and hurt.

The two men reported that the kidnappers had taken them out on the Navajo reservation, dumped them on the ground and kicked them. Minor said he asked for his fountain pen and was told he would not need it in hell. He said the men were well dressed and the cars were new. Their captors left them after pulling hoods over their heads, with a final warning, "Get out of here and stay out. If you ever come back we'll kill you." As soon as they got their hoods off, Minor and Levinson started to walk. They walked and walked. At last they found a deserted hogan and built a fire. About dawn they came to the hogan of Benny Tohé, a Navajo who cared for them and took them to Tohatchi in his car. Such in brief was their sensational story.

The Gallup case was no longer anything you could discuss on its merits. The plight of the miners gave way to a conflict between two schools of violent emotion, the Gallup "gang" and their friends, and the "outsiders" and their friends. Gallup could not get over its rage that outsiders dared peer into its private life, and dared publish their impressions in the press of the nation. Without question the outsiders had been haughty, self-righteous, and tactless. None of the labor and radical people who had come to the help of the miners assumed for a moment that New Mexico would give them a fair trial.

Gallup had a bad conscience because it had been caught red-handed in oppressing helpless people. If you have a neighbor who comes home drunk and beats up his children, there seems little point in telling him he should not act that way. He knows it already. He has a misery in his soul which he can do nothing about, and finds temporary relief in brutality. The misery in the soul of Gallup was the system of absentee landlords and the social irresponsibility which almost always goes with distant ownership.

To use publicity is to use force. It was the only

weapon the "outsiders" possessed, but they used it from the East Coast to the West until all of New Mexico grew restless and resentful. New Mexico did not think of itself as a capitalistic state. It has never been one except for the presence of a few corporations. Governor Tingley had been a worker in the railroad shops and carried a Federation of Labor card; his board of advisers were almost all self-made men. New Mexico wants to be the playground of the nation, and have millions and millions of tourists. It wants to show off the ruins left by vanished peoples, for those ruins are romantic, vacationists love to dig up bits of pottery. But the conflicts of today that may make the ruins of tomorrow are messy and repellent. To have their beloved state pictured in the press as furnishing the nation with another Sacco-Vanzetti or Scottsboro case was intolerable to New Mexicans.

The grievance of citizens in general had much more logic to it than the grievance of the Gallup "gang." The operators of the Gamerco mine had done their best to prevent employees from joining unions. Capital combines, but they denied labor the right for its own protection to follow suit. The Gamerco had the strength of great interests behind it, the miners had only the unions to turn to. Neither the town itself nor the Gamerco gave the miners a helping hand, and each day Chihuahuita festered the more. If you cannot put your house in order, outsiders are bound to step in and try to be of assistance. Gallup forgot that its peculiar ideas about housekeeping had only the previous year cost the state $90,000 for the National Guard alone.

The kidnapping came at an opportune moment for those interested in making class war the issue. The honest way Otero conducted the trial had dissipated any idea that the miners were to be framed. The labor lawyers and their supporters telegraphed everybody from the President down demanding military protection and congressional investigation. The word "demand" had never been in such demand.

Many people were skeptical about the kidnapping from the beginning. They regarded it as a fake show, staged to discredit the New Mexico authorities, make martyrs, arouse sympathy, secure donations. An old resident of Gallup commented, "Well, if those birds didn't precisely kidnap themselves, they certainly laid themselves open to trouble. We don't care much for eastern dudes and their women coming in here and telling us how bad we are. A few years ago they'd have danced to a brace of pistols. As it was, all they got was a good scare, and it was probably coming to 'em."

This Gallup resident's uncertainty as to how to regard the kidnapping, whether as really so or not, has been typical of New Mexico public opinion ever since. The members of the Gallup defense committee sitting in the hotel lobby at the time Levinson and Minor disappeared, later went out on the reservation with the

two men as a kind of unofficial investigating committee, taking with them several Navajo, an AP man, and
a detective. They reported that their findings indicated
that the kidnapping was real. On the other hand, Detective William Martin was sent by Chief E. J. House
of the State Police to the reservation to make an investigation; and nine days after the alleged kidnapping,
after examining all clues and taking the statements of
thirty-seven witnesses (so Martin told me himself), he
reported to Chief House that he had concluded it was
an imposition, and he recommended that no more public moneys be expended in connection with it. Like the
informal committee Martin had Navajo trackers with
him. Neither Martin's report nor the impression of the
committee was featured, if published at all, in the New
Mexico press, oddly enough; but word of them got
about and both probably played their part in the curious mixture of theory, opinion, conviction, insinuation,
charge and counter-charge that characterized the next
fortnight. A reader unacquainted with the landscape
might well wonder what earthly chance any investi-
gator, official or unofficial, would have of getting at the
facts of the case in so remote and unpeopled a spot.
But there seem to be Navajo everywhere on the reservation. You may think you are alone, with no other human being within fifty miles; yet a Navajo sheepherder
will be rolling his cigarette behind a rock within ear-
shot, aware of you all the time. Navajo are as accus-

tomed to read signs, whether footprints, tire tracks, marks of struggle, as other people are to read books. It happened too that on that portion of the reservation where the kidnapping was supposed to have taken place, it had rained on the fateful night, so that the episode was there to be read, for any Navajo or U. S. American who could read it correctly, for some days afterward.

On May 5, Judge Otero had arrived in Gallup on another case and found an atmosphere of recrimination. As he shaved and changed his shirt in his room at the Harvey house, he listened separately to Minor and Assistant District Attorney McIntosh, who had been calling each other liars, and tried to soothe the situation with humor and common sense. As Minor still feared assassination, the judge ordered Earl Irish to escort him and Levinson all the way to Santa Fe, and as the two men were suspicious of Gallup doctors, he telephoned his own physician to examine and ascertain the extent of their injuries.

A change of venue was Wirin's next demand. Judge Otero designated San Juan County on the Colorado line, an agricultural community speaking both English and Spanish, and with no labor troubles. The prosecution now disqualified Judge Otero—a privilege New Mexico law permits to either side without showing cause. As the two sides could not agree on a substitute, the supreme court appointed Judge James McGhee of

Chavez County. Judge McGhee considered the case too dangerous for any but the most experienced and able lawyers to handle. He appointed to defend the Gallup miners not untried boys but Hugh Woodward and John Simms of Albuquerque. Woodward had been United States attorney and Simms a justice of the state supreme court. If the miners had had all the money in the world it would not have bought them better counsel in New Mexico.

Mr. Levinson and Mr. Minor now took the train to New York, not to return. The Gallup defense committee, still determined to go outside the state boundaries for help, retained the firm of Donovan, Leisure, Newton, and Lombard of 2 Wall Street. This firm sent two young men recently out of law school, who asked only their expenses. They flew out, flew back, put up at good hotels, talked with New York by long distance daily, and even attended the trial.

With a long summer ahead, and money badly needed for the prisoners and ex-prisoners and their families, certain members of the organizations for the defense gave a good deal of money out of their own pockets. And the defense appealed for more through various benefits. The chairman of the Civil Liberties branch at Santa Fe was Michael Shepard, a war veteran with liberal inclinations, on a vacation from the New York publishing world. He was spending the summer in the Pojuaque valley, twenty miles north of

Santa Fe, with Allan Clark, the sculptor. Mr. and Mrs. Clark offered their place, the unusually beautiful Jacona Ranch, for a benefit tea. Clark had designed the big adobe house himself, and worked on its construction with the natives of the valley. The long cool rooms are lined with his serene heads and figures. The house is surrounded by sandy courts immaculately weeded. Behind it, on the edge of the dry river, a green cloud of cottonwoods rises against the bronze-red hill known as Santa Fe Marl. Hither on the appointed afternoon came writers, painters, dancers, Hollywood stars, from Taos and Santa Fe, and from the ranches in between, and the big ranches over towards Vegas. And also appeared people who had come out here for their health years before, and who had stayed on. And people of money who live out here because they like to. It was altogether a group who are in the life of the state, yet not of it, who have no political affiliations here and no invested money, and so are in that happy state of detachment when you freely speak your mind. The state likes to have these people live or visit here, for they spend money and lend the land luster in their fashion, and hook it onto the great world of wealth and culture. But it is often irritated by them, and sometimes is afraid of them.

It was such a group as had united and turned thumbs down when Santa Fe residents planned to buy for the plaza a replica of The Pioneer Mother, a group in cement which salutes you in town after town out West. They had said no, scornfully and decisively, when a group of women's clubs of the southern region had proposed to buy property in Santa Fe for an annual summer Chautauqua.

Marian Mitchell (Mrs. Langdon Mitchell) came to the benefit tea that afternoon, she who had acted in and had helped produce the first Ibsen play in London, in the nineties. She came into the patio with her picture hat and her trailing golden dress, and her stick, and the dignified beautiful walk that hides her arthritis, and I heard her say, of the Gallup miners, "Poor things, how dare they treat them so!" It seemed to me typical of the gathering, that distaste for human cruelty and violence. If such people were less transient and casual, their influence on public opinion might last longer and be more beneficial. But their cool aloofness from the local scene, the warmth of their adherence to human values, their war records, unquestioned patriotism, celebrity, or money, make them untouchables, and formidable at any given moment they care to declare themselves.

The trial began October 3 in Aztec, an elm-shaded town of big frame houses and gardens more like New England than New Mexico. It is a Mormon town, peaceful and attractive. That northern country is filled with fertile fields, fed by wide irrigation ditches. Compared with the rest of the state it is a land of plenty.

Its apples are well known. The Aztec jail was shaky, and so it was reinforced by an eight-foot barbed wire fence, and a bloodhound was chained to a tree. The bloodhound made friends with the prisoners; as Erna Fergusson said, he didn't know it was a class war. There was a squad of state troopers in new uniforms and Sam Browne belts. Judge McGhee's pistol clearly bulged from his coat tails, and he was attended by Mr. Sam McCue, also armed, and by two other guards. The weather was warm, the little courtroom stuffy. Amid the drone of bluebottle flies, everyone grew sleepy; it seemed as though the trial would stretch on to eternity. But Earl Irish leaned against a courtroom window and knocked the support out from under the sash. The window came down like a gunshot, and judge, jury, prisoners, counsel, and public leapt as one. The guilty trooper sheepishly braced the window up again, under the glare of indignant eyes.

Each morning dodgers appeared in the elm-shaded streets, "Save the Gallup workers. You may be next. Unite." One day a hundred carloads of Communists were reported coming up from Gallup. Defense attorneys chanced to ask a recess that day at the hour the Communists were supposed to be due. His Honor retired to his closely shuttered bedroom under guard of Sam McCue. Judge Simms and Mr. Woodward strolled in the plaza, but the only invading army they could report was a group of schoolboys with peashooters. The leftists were no less jittery. The more nervous whispered that McCue had planted a machine gun behind the fern in the window opposite the courthouse. When the reporter for the *Daily Worker* was threatened with contempt proceedings, her New York paper reported that she had been jailed. Judge McGhee was deluged with telegrams demanding her release, quite to his annoyance because the young woman sat as usual at the press table.

A jury was obtained without hitch. The state undertook to show that Navarro and Campos were held for housebreaking; that they were aided to escape by a rioting mob, that they or someone else had killed Carmichael and wounded two other officers. To make the whole mob responsible for whatever happened, the state also charged conspiracy. But cross-examination brought it out that the mob was composed largely of women and children, and so diminished the suggestion of its being very dangerous.

Hoy Boggess, the deputy, recited how he saw threatening gestures, how he hurled his tear-gas bomb, was struck down and knew nothing more until he saw Bobcat Wilson coming towards him doubled up with pain. But the state did not call Bobcat, and the defense attorneys did not discover at once that he and Boggess had left town soon after the latter's testimony. The state introduced a ballistics expert, and pistols in velvet cases. The defense admitted without dispute that these were the guns in question, and established neatly the fact that the bullet which killed Carmichael might have come from Boggess' own gun. It was their only interest in armament, for no other guns had been found, even in the bullying search through Chihuahuita.

Two women testified they had seen Leandro Velarde take an ice pick from the bib of his overalls and put it in the icebox. So Leandro's joke about the toothpick reappeared. District Attorney Chavez, resorting to his native tongue, tried to make the witnesses admit the possibility that Leandro might have said what the miners needed was ice picks. The witnesses did not think so.

Dee Roberts, the sheriff, was again the star witness. He told once more how he had seen his chief fall dead, and had at once shot and killed two men. He swore also to seeing Juan Ochoa coming at him with a claw hammer. No one else had seen that. And to seeing Ochoa and Avitia kicking and beating Hoy Boggess as he lay on the pavement. No one else had seen that, either. On cross-examination, he admitted that he had rounded up and held more than a hundred people, many of whom he had never seen; and that he had recognized only eight in the alley.

The defense moved the dismissal of all charges, but was overruled. It then put Manuel Avitia and Juan Ochoa on the stand in their own defense. Mr. Chavez asked Ochoa if he had organized the union, and if he were a Communist. To this the defense objected at once, for a man may incriminate himself, however innocent he is of crime, by admitting that he has united the unemployed, or that he belongs to a certain political party.

Judge Simms, though a New Mexican, belongs to the world of manner and manners which attended the benefit tea at Allan Clark's, and you don't forget him in a courtroom if you ever have the luck to see him. Nor do you forget Mr. Woodward, a veteran in the courts of justice, with rare good humor and complete reasonableness. They presented a remarkable defense to save from the electric chair ten men who could not be proven to have conspired, to have fired a fatal shot, to have aided prisoners to escape. Judge Simms was so effective in picturing poverty-stricken people caught in a wave of hate that Mr. McCue, his Honor's bodyguard, was heard to murmur, "My God, I wish he'd hush."

In the end no one was sent to the chair. The jury brought in a verdict of acquittal for seven men. The other three, Ochoa the leader of the miners, Avitia, and Leandro of the toothpick, were found guilty of second-degree murder, with a recommendation for clemency. Judge McGhee sentenced the three men to from forty-five to sixty years at hard labor.

Defense asked an appeal, and the Court allowed it.

That gentleman, having held in for many days, then let himself go and spoke his mind freely:

"The Court: . . . According to reports there has been a large amount of money raised for the defense of you men. These two attorneys from Mr. Donovan's office in New York say they have not received any of it. Mr. Augur, Mr. Woodward and Judge Simms have not received any of it, so somebody must have plenty of money to finance your appeal. . . . If necessary, you can show the supreme court that you don't have the money and can't get hold of this money that has been raised for you, and they will appoint someone to represent you. I hope that the members of the supreme court may be spared the abuse, the threats, and the attempted intimidation which has been practiced on me since my designation to sit in this case and which was heaped upon Judge Otero . . . until he was disqualified in the case; it seems after that time he became a good man again. The courts of the United States stand as a protection for the poor. Certainly only a small portion of the citizens of our country have any sympathy with the communistic cause. The Communists and those reds, agitators and anarchists who demand your release would demand your execution without trial. We don't operate our courts in New Mexico and the United States by mob rule. You prisoners have received as able defense as I have seen presented in any court, and I have been around courts since I was ten years old. I have never seen a more able defense, and it was because of this able defense that you and your co-defendants escaped the electric chair. Had it not been for the recommendation of the jury, I would have imposed the maximum sentence on you men. I hope that future governors, in the event this case is affirmed on appeal, will have the courage to do their duty and not release you unless they are convinced that an injustice was done in your conviction or that subsequent events justify executive clemency. That is all."

The supreme court, where Judge Simms and Mr. Woodward later appeared, reversed the judgment in regard to Leandro Velarde, the toothpick joker, and set him free. Manuel Avitia was pardoned in 1938, after serving two years of his sentence, and Juan Ochoa in 1939, after serving three years. That the case had such an issue is most certainly due to the fact that New Mexico has men and women determined to see justice prevail. Gallup is by far the biggest test in Americanism the Southwest has faced so far, and it leaves an impression in the main encouraging.

To insure continuance of such a tradition, the technique of impartiality in action might well be studied in the schools together with the partisan actions of both sides that endanger it. I hope the Gallup case will not be left to molder with old newspapers. For New Mexico and Arizona, at least, the record of the case is an eye-opening study of the various psychologies which belong to U. S. Americans. Out of this conflict of points of view blossomed, even if somewhat bedraggled, the American flower of fair play.

30. *Stories by Way of Epilogue*

THE INDIAN has his problems, which because they belong to him, belong also to us. Many of them our presence aggravates. But his sense of humor, his understanding of us and misunderstanding, his patience and wisdom, everything that makes him what he is, give the Southwest unceasing charm. The Navajo call Hitler the man who smells his mustache. Tony Lujan of Taos said to a boy of fourteen, fresh from an eastern school and full enough of the novelty of the Southwest to sleep with a revolver under his pillow, "I have a horse for you to break in." The boy saw the humor of the offer, but he also saw its friendliness. A teacher asked a young Navajo who had been home to the reservation, "How did you find your grandfather?" Surprised, the boy replied, "I didn't have to find my grandfather. I was born." Out at Ildefonso a white man said to an Indian, "I have no time," and the Indian replied, "There's none you don't have" (i.e., you have all there is of it). After the fiesta dance at San Felipe we were having supper by the river, and a boy from the pueblo came by and sat down with us. He was looking for an American boy who had promised to meet him and had not done so. "But I don't get mad at Mexican or white people. I don't get mad no matter what they do. My mother says it is no good to. Just be nice to everybody, she says—then *you* are all right."

It was a cloudless August day and we were watching the fiesta dance at a pueblo which had persisted for centuries in remarkably unpromising country. I was impressed by the fine physique and stature of five or six middle-aged male dancers. They appeared of different stock from the rest of the village, and I commented on the fact to Elizabeth Shepley Sergeant. She had spent some time in this pueblo and had been able to serve the people in various ways, and so knew them and their background. The men I spoke of were brothers, she told me, and their father had come years before from another tribe or pueblo. He lived on a side street near the plaza, and she led me to the house. There, sitting serenely in the sun outside his door, was a man of seventy or eighty, blind, but tall and well built out of the ordinary.

I have often thought of this old man since, and of the great happiness that must fill his bosom. For what must it be like to bring new life of one's own vigor to a time-worn and ailing village!

One night in 1924 when we were on our way to the intertribal ceremony in Gallup, Witter Bynner, Lynn

Riggs, Lewis Riley, and I climbed to the top of Acoma under the big stars, and when we got there five Indian youths were waiting for us, and stopped us. "What kind of people are you?" they asked. "Only dogs prowl at night." We had been thoughtless, and they were justified. But it was a rift in the long-suffering courtesy of the Pueblos, and struck us as curious. We exchanged cigarettes and began talking, and it came out that a friend of theirs had lately been in trouble in Santa Fe. He had come to town with a wagon and hitched his horses at what he thought a suitable place. A policeman arrested him for interfering with traffic. He had a bewildering time extricating himself from this difficulty, and nobody in Santa Fe came to his assistance.

Our American preoccupation with car, toilet facilities, and radio have their effect on the Indians. Their scorn shows it, but they show it in other ways, too. Jane Henderson Baumann grew fond of a little boy during her days at the pueblo, and once his parents left him with her when they were taking a trip. He did not want to be alone, would not even go into the bathroom by himself. But the bathroom interested him more than anything else in the house. When the time came for him to go home he felt badly. He walked from room to room by himself, for the first time, and entered the bathroom. He lifted the lid from the toilet seat, and then lifted the oval seat itself and put one hand through it to grasp the other hand, and the two shook hands fervently while the little boy made a guttural melancholy address of farewell.

Three Santa Fe boys (Charles Schmidt, Bob Well, and Tony Long) celebrated their graduation from high school by a three weeks' trip through the Navajo reservation and the country north of it. The lilacs were in blossom in the Mormon towns, and the boys were impressed by the luxuriance of the bushes. They could smell the towns sometimes before they saw them. At Cedar City over the Utah line, they went to the movie, and Bob Well lost his billfold with a twenty-dollar bill in it. He did not discover the loss till they were turning in, in their bedrolls. Early the next morning they went back to the theater, wondering whether they could find anyone to let them in. But the door was not locked. So they went in, and located the place where they had sat the night before. Bob struck a match and found his pocketbook on the floor under his seat.

The Demchek murder case brought to light a group of Czechs unassimilated by the state and having little connection with it. Because of the wildness of the country there are more such groups than we know. Barela Mesa is an immense place on the Colorado boundary, and none too accessible. The Czechs live up there on their ranches, raise sheep, cattle, and chickens, work at times in the mines near Raton, and go hunting. Barela Mesa is excellent hunting, as is also Bear Canyon near-by; but few hunters like to hunt there. The Czechs are an unknown quantity. They don't mix, and mind their own business; but they are hard workers, and the few who know them consider them fine people.

While investigating the case, Detective Martin went to the mesa in a November snowstorm and stuck at the top. He went on foot to the first house he could find, and asked the Czech to harness his team and drag him through the drifts. The storm continued several days, and he stayed with this family. Each day the Czech drove him where he wanted to go. When about to return to Raton, Martin asked the man how much he owed him. "The state will pay you a fair price." "The state pay me?" This fact interested the Czech. "Yes." "I charge the state only half-dollar a day." "You can charge more than that, for your horses." "No. Half-dollar a day. The state arrest me for bootlegger. It no put me in jail, gave me suspend' sentence, let me go. I'm friend of the state."

In 1843 the Mexican Republic granted Charles Beaubien and Guadalupe Miranda a stretch of land on the northernmost boundary of New Mexico. It was intended as a buffer against the encroachment of the United States. Mexican law permitted the granting of only eleven square leagues, about thirty-three square miles, to one petitioner, so that twice that extent of land would be all this particular grant could include. In 1857 the Surveyor General of the United States and in 1860 the Congress confirmed the grant as "good and valid under Mexican law." Beaubien died in 1864 and left most of the grant to his daughter Luz. His son-in-law Lucien Maxwell bought out the other heirs. In 1869 Maxwell applied for a survey because squatters were beginning to come in. He claimed some two million acres of land. The Secretary of the Interior, Sunset Cox, threw out this stupendous claim and ruled that the grant was limited to the original twenty-two square leagues (about 97,000 acres). In 1870 Maxwell sold the vague territory of which he was overlord to three Colorado business men for $650,000. They at once resold it for $1,350,000 to an English syndicate called the Maxwell Land Grant and Railway Co. A group of gilded youths came from London with blooded hounds, five grand pianos, and a group of stuffed Bengal tigers to take over the estate and resist the squatters. After the Civil War, veterans of both the Union and Confederate armies were moving west, and the law stated the squatter's right to land on which he paid taxes for ten years.

The English owners undertook a new survey of the land. It is widely believed (though it has never been proven) that twenty leagues square looked better to them than twenty square leagues, and that they set back the four corners of the boundary. In any case the government surveyors, whom they entertained in princely fashion at Maxwell's great mansion at Cimarron, set their seal to a survey that showed some two million acres.

Once when an old resident of Trinidad, A. W. Archibald, was asked if he could remember when Fisher's Peak was a hole in the ground, he replied, "No, but I remember well when they moved it forty miles north." Fisher's Peak rises just that distance north of Tinaja Peak, which looks like it and which old-timers say was the original northeast corner.

The English owners with the new survey and U. S. law on their side now proceeded to make trouble for the squatters. The squatters argued that the extension of the original grant to two million acres constituted the biggest land grab in the history of the West. The Squatters' War followed, culminating in a battle at Stonewall. Most of the settlers there were veterans of the Civil War, but they were defeated, and their leaders killed, by the "forces of law and order," the English owners.

Andrew Duling was asked in court about his ranch. "You own this ranch, Mr. Duling?"

"I presume so."

"You presume so? Haven't you got title?"

"Oh, yes, I've got several titles."

"Several titles to the same land? Please explain that, sir."

"You see when I came West I bought that land from a settler who lived there. I dug a ditch, built a house, made other improvements. Surveyors came along and said I didn't own it, it was government land. So I filed on it and bought it again. Then the Maxwell Land Grant informed me it was theirs. They brought suit; some of my neighbors resisted, I saw friends murdered. There were only three possibilities—to fight, leave, or buy again. I bought again."

This is a story for those Southwesterners to think about who talk excitedly about the race question, oppressed minorities, and subject peoples. Is it ever a question of race? Is it not rather of power, and of poverty?

A Navajo woman named Mrs. Bryan was discussing the European war with Maria Chabot. "Why do they want to kill each other over there—because a man kills another man why should somebody else kill him?"

Maria could not answer this question. It is not easy to answer.

Mrs. Bryan said, "Before you white people came with your laws, when a Navajo killed another Navajo, then all his family had to save. They had to save a long time, because they had to pay for it."

We do not explain our customs and the reasons for them clearly enough to the Navajo. We act as though he had been a close student of our economic life for generations. A Navajo applied for a job on the highway and was informed he could not get it without a Social Security card. He talked about this card afterwards, trying to grasp what it might be. "We have to buy it. I don't know how much people have to pay for it. I don't have any of that card, so I don't have any of that job. You have to send for it to Albuquerque to Social Security Boards and Company."

The Navajo are patriotic. When it is shown at the movies the flag excites them. They enjoy movies, particularly programs of two or more "features" and six or seven "shorts," and will sit from seven o'clock to twelve without falling asleep, just like many urban movie-goers. At their Tribal Council in June, 1940, they passed patriotic resolutions. "Whereas, there exists no purer concentration of Americanism than among the first Americans . . . we hereby serve notice that any un-American movement among our people will be resented and dealt with severely. . . ." The phrasing sounds more like Superintendent Fryer than the Navajo, but various delegates made speeches.

Paul Begay of District 2 said, "The proposition that we are talking about, the subject of defending our country and getting ready, seems to have sort of given me an air that stands me out prominently. It seems that it has lifted me and I am standing on something firmer than I realized before. Those things you talked about tonight, I want to express my appreciation and thanks that you should all have the same attitude and that you have all stated your willingness to defend your country."

William Goodluck of District 18 said, "During the World War I noticed in one of the papers a picture of an eagle. When I saw it I thought, whoever put that on paper, the picture of it the way it was, must have been a wise man. That picture was an eagle fluttering over a chicken, and the explanation was that the enemy was represented by the chicken and that our eagle had subdued it and was ready to devour. I would like to see us be that same eagle and pick up that same chicken that is now making a lot of trouble."

Spanish pronouns and negatives give U. S. Americans real trouble, and Spanish Americans have trouble too with our negatives and pronouns. The following are fatalities on the native side of the combat, as you can observe in talk along the road and in the little villages.

"Me thank you too much for my kindness."

"I give you too much thanks for my kindness."

"Me thank you too much. Maybe some time you won't come back again, I hope."

"When I tol' him for a job she asked me no."

A friend of mine showed a native a campaign leaflet purporting to list the relatives of a certain senator who hold government jobs. The native's comment was, "He is a good man. He takes care of his family." Another native, speaking of politics in his county, said, "In San Miguel we honor the dead. When election day comes we let them vote."

Natives do not complain much over serious matters, such as blindness. But over the lesser matters which it would be presumptuous to regard as the will of God since it belittles Him to imagine He would spend much time thinking up annoyances for His children, they do complain, and not sotto voce. Dr. Warren, a chiropractor, says a native came to his office complaining that his arm was "inflamed." The arm was tied up in a cow-dung poultice, and the doctor did not like to disturb this poultice. So he X-rayed the arm. What he found was outside his province, a fracture, a "lovely" example of that kind of mishap. He said to the patient, "What has happened to you lately?" "Nawthing." "You must have done something to that arm. Did you fall on it?" "No, maybe my horse he throw me other day."

This reluctance to see a cause and effect relation in events is also not uncommon among native people, and accounts for many things they say and do. After all, they contend, how can you be sure it was that? And quite often, how can you?

Outside of politics and matrimony it is not easy to find a native funny story that U. S. Americans also consider funny. The rather grim one that follows is such a story, but if American hearers have any guesses as to whom or what the big husky boy symbolizes, the story probably sobers them more than it amuses them:

The old man came home badly beaten. The boy, "Papacito, que te pasa?" (Papa, what happened to you?)

"I was passing a house up above here and a boy came out. He said, 'I'm going to hit you.' He hit me."

The boy, "Bueno, papacito, vamos por allá." (We'll go over there and see about this.)

They went over there and knocked on the door. A big husky boy came out.

First boy, "Now you're not going to hit my papacito."

Second boy, "No?" And he knocked the old man flat.

First boy, "I bet you won't do it again."

He knocked him flat again.

First boy, "Papacito, vamos, le va matar!" (Papa, let's get out of here, he's going to kill you.)

My friend Salas, who is thirty-eight years old and comes of an old Spanish family, told me that when he was a ten-year-old boy he was driving in a buggy with his grandfather and little brother down the Jemez valley, and they crossed the wide dry wash over to the pueblo of Sia. A little Indian girl was crying, and the people said she had been crying for a long time. Salas's grandfather said to her parents, "Let me take this child back with me to my ranch [near Albuquerque] and get a doctor." The Indians would not agree to it. He offered finally to buy her from them. The parents after long consideration and with tears accepted the offer, and he gave a jug of wine and a pail of corn for her. Salas said she cried all the way to the ranch. The physician came and discovered that she had a spinal injury, to cure which nothing much could be done. But she lived, and in a fashion got over it. Salas and his little brother grew up with her, and were fond of her. In her twenties she married a mechanic and went to Chicago to live, and she is still living there.

Spanish people and Indians know a good deal about one another. They have learned it through centuries of war and slavery and living near together. The elder Salas understood the predicament of the parents of the suffering child. They were facing a problem they could do nothing about. He understood also how to solve it for them in a way that for a variety of reasons they would find, if not acceptable to them, at least the best way out for the child.

Visitors speeding through the piñon country on the new highways may not realize that this region is woven over with human associations from the earliest times and wears a complex web of incident and fancy in countless myths, legends, and stories. The Indians are sun-worshipers; the Zuñi word for life is daylight. The great hero, the great villain, is the sun, and the Pueblos have many tales of his relations with men and with the daughters of men. So have the other tribes. In a creation-myth of the White Mountain Apache, the sun's son seeks his father's home and is hidden by the wife of the sun, who is not his mother. When the sun returns at dusk, his wife says to him, "You have always told me that when you traveled you never did anything wrong, but this is not so, because your boy came here today." Such a tale has a Greek sound, and you often think of the ancient Greeks in Indian country.

For those who know Indian stories, the butterflies, birds, moths, grasshoppers, chipmunks, coyotes, along the road form the dramatis personae of an endless entertainment. Even the humble road runner, which impresses everybody as nondescript and devoid of "it," is portrayed in all his flatness in a story about his being jilted by Quail Girl and Yellow Warbler Girl. "All the different kinds of birds were like people in those days," says the story teller, to let you know old tales can have a modern slant. These primitive stories contain pointed repartee, between skunk and bear for example, or between mescal and white-tailed deer. Wolf and mountain lion are not good friends; their technique of depredation differs. Wolf says, "You crawl along on your belly and hide yourself. That is why you have sores on your belly and on your knees. That is the way you hunt." Mountain lion answers, "You chase the deer all over and get them hot. Then you kill them and eat the meat when it is hot. It is no good that way." Navajo tales of wild turkey and coyote have special zest; both have been shaped into truly great characters through the generations. It was Turkey who first brought corn to the Apache; he shook it out of his feathers. He pretends not to remember the episode, and this is a source of great mirth to the listeners. Indians comment audibly and in disgust at Coyote's misdeeds when they appear in the tales. He is a peculiarly disagreeable character, while Turkey always wins you, even when his deeds are hardly ethical.

With the native people it is the saint rather than the sun or the animals of whom the stories are told. Most of these stories are narratives of the kindly and invisible friends who are always at hand, and who do not desert you when you fall on evil days. A santo is a painting of a saint, flat and generally on wood, and at times in a glass case. The native people in the Cienega valley have a santo of San José in their church, about which Leonora Curtin tells me they relate the following: Five generations or more ago, a Cienega youth went down the Chihuahua trail to Durango to be trained as a priest. During his years in Old Mexico he ran across a fine santo of San José, in Zacatecas I think it was. He bought him, took him back to Cienega, and placed him in the church. At that time the church stood on ground that belonged to a wealthy and grasping rico. This rico in the course of time decided to move to a hacienda he owned near Bernalillo. On Sunday morning when the village folk went to mass they found no santo of San José. Suspecting what had happened, they surged angrily down the highway, and they had not gone far when they came upon a wagon and two dead oxen. On the wagon was the santo; he had grown so heavy in his reluctance to leave the people who loved and needed him that the oxen perished trying to pull him. Two striplings went into a near-by farmhouse and borrowed a daybed. Without assistance they lifted San José from the wagon to the daybed (he had grown light for them) and bore him back to his home, while the people followed singing. The men began at once to build a new church for him, and two generations later he was taken to a third church, the one in which he now abides. Each day on his feast day, December 19, the people walk around the church singing and giving thanks for his unfailing protection.

Index

Abeyta, Pablo, 45
Abreu, Don Ramón, 177, 180
Abreu, Don Santiago, 177, 180
Acequia Madre, 5
Adaptation, human, in Southwest: lack of water, 3 ff., 97; regional weather, 11 ff.; shifts of altitude, 23, 30; diet, 18, 93; corn culture, 70 ff.; Oñate's horses, cattle, and sheep, 83-85; personal acceptance necessary, Núñez, 32-36; Kit Carson, 147-150; Bronson Cutting, 143-145; Billy the Kid over-adapted, 185-187; ricos failed to adapt to wealth and privilege, 95; human body an instrument of adaptation, 211-214; our fate partly in the keeping of one another, 214
Adventures in Respiration, 20
Albuquerque, N. M., 5, passim
Alexander, Dr. and Mrs. Henry S. A., 15
Allen, Captain James, 158
"All right," feeling of, 260
Altitude, in relation to rainfall, 6; effect of, on people, not explored, 19-21
American Civil Liberties Union, 280, 293
American Men of Science, 17
Angel, Judge Frank W., 187
Apache Indians, 28, 59-60, 171
Archibald, A. W., 309
Arizona, 3, passim

Arizona, northern, nature and difficulties of, 155, 156, 163, 164
Armer, Mrs. Laura Adams, 254
Augur, Wheaton, 281, 285
Avitia, Manuel, 278 ff.
Ayer, Edward E., 174
Aztec, N. M., 295

Bancroft Library, 181
Bangs, Samuel, 176
Barella, Maria, 5
Barreiro, Don Antonio, 177
Bartol, Mrs. Julia, 286
Baudelaire, 128
Baumann, Gustave, 13, 80, 202-205
Baumann, Mrs. Gustave (Jane Henderson), 63-68, 305
Bayliss, Prof. William, 20
Beaubien, Charles, and daughter Luz, 184, 307, 308
Begay, Paul, 311
Bellamy, Edward, 166
Benally, Lee, 246
Bernalillo, N. M., 8, 52
Bickel, William J., 276, 284
Billy the Kid, his story significant, could be told the tourist significantly, 184-190
Bill Williams Mountain, 265
Blue Forest, 202
Boggess, Hoy, 277, 297, 298
Boudousquié, Antoine, 179
Bowman, Mrs. Bessie, 210

319